KARMIC RELATIONSHIPS VOL. III

KARMIC RELATIONSHIPS

Esoteric Studies

Vol. III

RUDOLF STEINER

Eleven lectures given at Dornach, Switzerland, between 1st July and 8th August, 1924

Translated by George Adams
with revisions by D. S. Osmond

RUDOLF STEINER PRESS

Rudolf Steiner Press
Hillside House, The Square
Forest Row, East Sussex
RH18 5ES

www.rudolfsteinerpress.com

First edition 1957
Second edition 1977
Reprinted 2002, 2009

Originally published in German under the title *Esoterische Betrachtungen karmischer Zusammenhänge, Dritter Band* (volume 237 in the *Rudolf Steiner Gesamtausgabe* or Collected Works) by Rudolf Steiner Verlag, Dornach. This authorized translation is published by permission of the Rudolf Steiner Nachlassverwaltung, Dornach

A catalogue record for this book is available from the British Library

ISBN 978 1 85584 216 8

Printed and bound in Great Britain by
4edge Limited, Hockley, Essex

SUMMARY OF CONTENTS

PAGE

Extract from a lecture given 22nd June, 1924 11

I

Intellectualism and the mood of soul which preceded it: men received the thoughts into themselves from the cosmic ether. As late as the early Middle Ages this old conception persisted in personalities influenced on the one side by Arabism and on the other by Aristotelianism. For the civilisation of Europe a special impulse towards the development of the Spiritual Soul was necessary. Two spiritual streams in conflict: the quasi-Arabian philosophers and the Dominican Scholastics who, as the representatives of individualism, fight against them. Intense inner conflicts at the time of this struggle to make possible the development of the Spiritual Soul and to uphold the reality of individual Thinking. 13

1st July, 1924

II

Forces of karmic preparation in the cosmos. The former incarnations of a man work on his later incarnations as a spiritual instinct within the Ego; after death he becomes objectively conscious of the experiences undergone on earth. The web of karmic relationships. The transmutation of the earthly deeds of men into the heavenly deeds of souls. When two human beings are working together something takes place as between the two, transcending the individual experiences of either. The connection of what happens in the human world on earth with what goes on in the spiritual worlds above is at most established for the ordinary consciousness when sacred spiritual actions are brought into the physical world of sense. The heavenly deeds and consequences of certain happenings fall like a fine rain into the mirror-images of thought on earth. But the shades, the very real ghosts of the 19th century move about among the men of the present day who are enticed by the Ahrimanic trend of the age. 29

4th July, 1924

III

The connection between human life on earth and that which goes on in the cosmos. Whatever happens here on earth has its corresponding counterpart in the spiritual worlds. This comes to expression in the writing of the stars. What are the spiritual, cosmic realities underlying such a community as the Anthroposophical Society? By what predisposition is a soul led to Anthroposophy?—A longing for Christ accompanies many souls from their pre-earthly life into their present life on earth: they strive again to know Christ as a Being of the Sun. Christian experience mingles with the conceptions of ancient Paganism. In many souls influences are present which make it possible for men to fall victim to the temptations of Lucifer and Ahriman. 43

6th July, 1924

IV

Two groups are to be distinguished in the Anthroposophical Movement: the one with a more inward need of the heart to place Christ in the central point, the other finding great satisfaction in knowing Him from the aspect of cosmology and of earthly and human history. The origins of this grouping go back to the times of the Atlantean Oracles. For those souls who come to Anthroposophy to-day, that incarnation is particularly important which falls into the early centuries after Christ. Some human souls have had many, others comparatively few past incarnations on the earth. Souls of the one group, taken as a whole, received Christianity in those early centuries chiefly through their intellect; the others received the impulses paramountly into their will. Experiences in the life between death and a new birth of the mighty Imaginations enacted as a supersensible spiritual action in the first half of the 19th century. 57

8th July, 1924

V

The common element in the soul-condition of the two groups in the first Christian centuries was a feeling, slight and delicate but present nevertheless, between falling asleep and waking, of the Spiritual working and weaving in external Nature, and of the instreaming of spirituality in the light-filled spaces of the cosmos. Perception of the innocence of Nature's being. Then men began to ponder about the depth of the forces that bring forth the good and evil in the human soul. This mood of soul arose especially among those who received knowledge and teachings from the East. (' Bulgars '—human beings who were most strongly touched by this opposition of the good and evil spiritual powers. Heretics). Then came the time when vision of the rainbow-shining glory over the plants, the desire-nature about the animals, faded away; between falling asleep and waking the whispered language of the spiritual worlds grew fainter but the Spiritual could still be spoken of as of something known to men; in the following time, the feeling of the souls in their life after death was that upon earth the evening twilight of the Logos had set in. With this is connected the rise of the Catechism; the Mass in its totality becomes exoteric instead of being divided, as formerly, into an exoteric and an esoteric portion. The fundamental feeling of the souls in the spiritual world between the 7th and the 20th century was: Christ is no longer being recognised in His true nature; the sacred ceremony is no longer understood. This feeling intensified their sense of the need for a new Christ-experience on the earth. 71

11th July, 1924

VI

High places of knowledge, relics of the ancient Mysteries, were present until the 7th or 8th century A.D. In those centres men did not speak of abstract laws of Nature but of the creative power of the Goddess Natura. Then the delicate but living connection with the spiritual world faded but the old teachings were still cultivated in certain centres whose impulses only came to an end in the 12th or 13th century. Knowledge concerning the four Elements, the Planetary System, the 'Cosmic Ocean', the secrets of the ' I ', were cultivated until the turn of the 14th–15th century. The School of Chartres and its teachers. Towards the end of the 12th century, such teachings were still cultivated in the University of Orleans. Platonists and Aristotelians. Brunetto Latini. At the beginning of the 13th century a supremely important ' exchange of ideas ' took place in the spiritual world with the aim of bringing about a new spirituality on earth. A wonderful co-operation between souls working from above and those who were below on earth was the result. Into this spiritual atmosphere true Rosicrucianism was able to pour its influence. 85

13th July, 1924

VII

The manipulation of the intellect by the individual, personal man leads him to freedom of will. In the first Christian centuries, until the 8th or 9th, the Cosmic Intelligence was flowing down from the heavens to the earth. Scholasticism: a wrestling of mankind for a clear understanding of the Intelligence that is pouring in. The Spiritual Soul, and with it the Intelligence, begins to become part of humanity. Rosicrucian wisdom consisted in this, that one had a certain clarity of understanding for these facts. In the domain of the Sun, Michael gathered around him the souls who then, at the beginning of the 15th century, were united in the supersensible School of Michael. From now onwards the Michael principle was to be developed through the Intelligence of the human soul itself until the beginning of the new Michael Age on earth at the end of the 19th century. The great crisis from the beginning of the 15th century until our day is the battle of Ahriman against Michael. Ahriman wants to make the former Cosmic Intelligence altogether earthly. The carrying over of the Cosmic Intelligence into the system of nerves and senses (the head-organisation) in man is experienced from the spiritual world as though a cosmic thunderstorm were taking its course. Such an event had last taken place in Atlantean time when the Cosmic Intelligence, while remaining cosmic, had taken possession of the hearts of men. Through spiritualisation of the intellect, the head-man must now again become a heart-man. The end of the century. 101

28th July, 1924

VIII

The previous Michael dominion, its cosmopolitan stamp and its aim: the consciousness that in spite of the Fall, man can after all ascend to the Divinity. Since the 8th or 9th century the Cosmic Intelligence has passed from the hands of Michael into the hands of men. Conflict between the Scholastics and the Mahommedan followers of Aristotelian learning. In the last Michael age an atmosphere of discouragement had come over the ancient

Mysteries; it was an age of great trial and probation. The word of Michael at that time was: Man must reach the Pan-Intelligence, he must take hold of the Divine upon earth in sinless form. In the new Michael age men will have to become aware of the way of their salvation, to realise that they must rescue themselves from Ahriman's aim to take possession of the Intelligence that has come into their hands. Anthroposophists must learn to realise that the cosmos to-day is engaged in this battle of Ahriman against Michael. Earthly reflection in Raymond of Sabunda of the teachings of Michael in the supersensible. It is a Michael impulse to lead men again to the point where they will read in the Book of Nature, not only in the Book of Revelation. 119

1st August, 1924

IX

The Michael impulses are of a kind to enter deeply and intensely into the whole being of man, hence into his physical karma. The time of the great crisis. The Michael impulses are fraught with great decisions. Human beings who in the present incarnation receive the Michael impulses through Anthroposophy are thereby preparing their whole being in such a way that these Michael impulses enter even into the forces that are otherwise determined merely by the connections of race and nation. The finer, more intimate connections of life must be observed; they extend even into the realms of the Angeloi. While the Michael community is being formed here on earth, the kingdom of the Angeloi is being turned into a twofold kingdom, a kingdom of Angeloi with an upward tendency, and one with a downward tendency. The intellectualism prevailing everywhere to-day is spiritual nourishment for the Ahrimanic Powers. The possibilities for Ahriman to take a hand in civilisation have become ever greater and greater. A diminution or diversion of consciousness in a human being gives Ahriman the possibility to incorporate himself and to work out of that human being. The age is fraught with mighty decisions. 133

3rd August, 1924

X

In the karmic impulse impelling a man towards the Spiritual are summed up all the experiences undergone in the way described before the souls descended into the present earthly life. Inner initiative of soul is demanded of the anthroposophist. Undermining of initiative through the materialistic intellectualism that is so widespread to-day. Undetermined fear of life. Materialism holds good of physical life only. The tragedy in the karma of men who cannot find their way to spirituality. The time will come when in human beings who are taken hold of by the Spirit in this earthly incarnation, the Spirit will reveal its own power to form the physiognomy, to shape the whole form of man. To those who stand in the field of materialism to-day it will be demonstrated that the Spirit is creative, for they will behold it in outer form and feature. Ahriman's striving to tear the Intelligence from Michael. The Ahrimanic spirits cannot incarnate but can temporarily incorporate themselves and so work in the souls of men. Ahriman has in this way actually appeared as an author. (See end of next lecture. Nietzsche's *Anti-Christ* and *Ecce Homo*). 147

4*th August*, 1924

XI

Battle waged by the Schoolmen of the Dominican Order to maintain and uphold the personal immortality of man. Averroes declared a heretic. To-day we have to say: " In the sense in which man has become immortal, as to his Spiritual Soul, he has indeed attained immortality—the continued consciousness of personality after passing through the gate of death—but he has attained this only since the time when a Spiritual Soul took up its abode in earthly man." The Sun-Intelligence of Michael and the Planetary Intelligences. In the 9th century A.D., with the descent of the Cosmic Intelligence into men, the Sun-Intelligence of Michael and the Planetary Intelligences gradually came into cosmic opposition one with another. In the Ecumenical Council of 869 A.D. the signal was given for an overwhelming event in the spiritual world above: a split among the Angels who guide human souls, leading to disorder in the karma of men. This is the chaotic element in the history of recent times. With the penetration of Michael to earthly rulership, Michael brings the power which is to bring order again into the karma of those who have gone with him. The restoration of the truth in karma. The mission of Anthroposophy. ... 161

8*th August*, 1924

EDITOR'S PREFACE

During the year 1924, before his illness in September, Rudolf Steiner gave over eighty lectures, published under the title *Karmic Relationships: Esoteric Studies*, to members of the Anthroposophical Society in the following places: Dornach, Berne, Zürich, Stuttgart, Prague, Paris, Breslau, Arnhem, Torquay and London. English translations of these lectures are contained in the following volumes of the series:

Vols. I to IV. Lectures given in Dornach (49).
Vol. V. Lectures given in Prague (4) and Paris (3).
Vol. VI. Lectures given in Berne (2) Zürich (1) Stuttgart (3) Arnhem (3).
Vol. VII. Lectures given in Breslau (9).
Vol. VIII. Lectures given in Torquay (3) and London (3).

All these lectures were given to members of the Anthroposophical Society only and were intended to be material for study by those already familiar with the fundamental principles of Anthroposophy. The following extract from the lecture of 22nd June, 1924 (see Vol. II) calls attention to the need for exactitude when passing on such contents:

"The study of problems connected with karma is by no means easy and the discussion of anything that has to do with the subject entails—or ought at any rate to entail—a sense of deep responsibility. Such study is in truth a matter of penetrating into the most profound mysteries of existence, for within the sphere of karma and the course it takes lie those processes which are the basis of the other phenomena of world-existence, even of the phenomena of nature... These difficult and weighty matters entail grave consideration of every word and every sentence spoken here, in order that *the limits within which the statements are made shall be absolutely clear...*"

The attention of readers is called to the fact that the fundamental explanations given by Rudolf Steiner of the laws and conditions of karma are contained in Vol. I of the series. Knowledge of the earlier lectures should therefore be regarded as an essential basis for study of those contained in the later volumes.

THE KARMIC RELATIONSHIPS
OF THE
ANTHROPOSOPHICAL MOVEMENT

I

Introduction to these Studies on Karma

For those of you who are able to be here to-day I wish to give a kind of interlude in the studies we have been pursuing for some time. What I shall say to-day will serve to illustrate and explain many a question that may emerge out of the subjects we have treated hitherto. At the same time it will help to throw light on the mood-of-soul of the civilisation of the present time.

For years past, we have had to draw attention to a certain point of time in that evolution of civilisation which is concentrated mainly in Europe. The time I mean lies in the 14th or 15th century or about the middle of the Middle Ages. It is the moment in the evolution of mankind when intellectualism begins—when men begin mainly to pay attention to the intellect, the life of thought, making the intellect the judge of what shall be thought and done among them.

Since the age of the intellect is with us to-day, we can certainly gain a good idea of what intellectualism is. We need but experience the present time, to gain a notion of what came to the surface of civilisation in the 14th and 15th century. But as to the mood of soul which preceded this, we are no longer able to feel it in a living way. People who study history nowadays generally project what they are accustomed to see in the present time, back into the historic past, and they have little idea how altogether different men were in mind and spirit before the present epoch. Even when they let the old documents speak for themselves, they largely read into them the way of thought and outlook of the present.

To spiritual-scientific study many a thing will appear altogether differently. Let us turn our gaze for example to those historic personalities who were influenced on the one hand from the side of Arabism, from the civilisation of Asia —influenced by what lived and found expression in the Mahommedan religion, while on the other hand they were influenced by Aristotelianism. Let us consider these personalities, who found their way in course of time through Africa to Spain, and deeply influenced the thinkers of Europe down to Spinoza and even beyond him. We gain no real conception of them if we imagine their mood of soul as though they had been like men of the present time with the only difference that they were ignorant of so and so many things subsequently discovered. (For roughly speaking, this is how they are generally thought of to-day). The whole way of thought and outlook, even of the men who lived in the above described stream of civilisation as late as the 12th century A.D., was altogether different from that of to-day.

To-day, when man reflects upon himself, he feels himself as the possessor of Thoughts, Feelings, and impulses of Will which lead to action. Above all, man ascribes to *himself* the 'I think,' the 'I feel' and the 'I will.'

But in the personalities of whom I am now speaking, the 'I think' was by no means yet accompanied by the same feeling with which we to-day would say 'I think.' This could only be said of the 'I feel' and the 'I will.' In effect, these human beings ascribed to their own person only their Feeling and their Willing. Out of an ancient background of culture, they rather lived in the sensation 'It thinks in me' than that they thought 'I think.' Doubtless they thought 'I feel,' 'I will,' but they did not think 'I think' in the same measure. On the other hand they said to themselves —and what I shall now describe was an absolutely real conception to them:—In the Sublunary Sphere, there live the thoughts. The thoughts are everywhere within this sphere, which is determined when we imagine the Earth at a certain point, and the Moon at another, followed by Mercury, Venus, etc. They not only conceived the Earth as a dense and rigid cosmic mass, but as a second thing belonging to it they conceived the Lunar Sphere, reaching up to the Moon. And as we say, 'In the air in which we breathe is oxygen,' so did these people say (it is only forgotten now that it ever was so):—'In the Ether which reaches up to the Moon, there are the thoughts.' And as we say 'We breathe-in the oxygen of the air,' so did these people say—not 'We breathe-in the thoughts'—but 'We perceive the thoughts, receive them into ourselves.' They were conscious of the fact that they received the thoughts.

To-day, no doubt, a man can also familiarise himself with such an idea as a theoretic concept. He may even understand it with the help of Anthroposophy, but as soon as it becomes a question of practical life he forgets it. For then at once he has this rather strange idea, that the thoughts spring forth within himself—which is just as though he were to think that the oxygen he receives in breathing were not received by him but sprang forth from within him.

For the personalities of whom I am now speaking, it was a profound feeling and an immediate experience: 'I have not my own thoughts as my own possession. I can not really say, I think. Thoughts exist, and I receive them unto myself.'

Now we know that the oxygen of the air circulates through our organism in a comparatively short time. We count these cycles by the pulse-beat. This happens quickly. The men of whom I am now speaking did indeed imagine the receiving of thoughts as a kind of breathing, but it was a very slow breathing. It consisted in this: At the beginning of his earthly life, man becomes capable of receiving the thoughts. As we hold the breath within us for a certain time—between our in-breathing and out-breathing—so did these men conceive a certain fact, as follows: They imagined that they held the thoughts within them, yet only in the sense in which we hold the oxygen which belongs to the outer air. They imagined that they held the thoughts during the time of their earthly life, and breathed them out again—out into the cosmic spaces—when they passed through the gate of death.

Thus it was a question of in-breathing—the beginning of life; holding the breath—the duration of earthly life; out-breathing—the sending-forth of the thoughts into the universe.

Men who had this kind of inner experience felt themselves in a common atmosphere of thought with all others who had the same experience. It was a common atmosphere of thought reaching beyond the earth, not only a few miles, but as I said, up to the orbit of the moon.

This idea was wrestling for the civilisation of Europe at that time. It was trying to spread itself ever more and more, impelled especially by those Aristotelians who came from Asia into Europe along the path I have just indicated. Let us suppose for a moment that it had really succeeded. What would then have come about?

In that case, my dear friends, that which was destined after all to find expression in the course of earthly evolution, could never have come to expression in the fullest sense: I mean, the Spiritual Soul. The human beings of whom I am now speaking, stood in the last stage of evolution of the Intellectual or Mind-Soul. In the 14th and 15th century, the Spiritual Soul was to arise—the Spiritual Soul, which, if it found extreme expression, would lead all civilisation into intellectualism.

The population of Europe in its totality, in the 10th, 11th and 12th centuries, was by no means in a position merely to submit to the outpouring of a conception such as was held by the men whom I have now described. For if they had done so, the evolution of the Spiritual Soul would not have come about. Though it was determined in the councils of the Gods that the Spiritual Soul should evolve, nevertheless it could not evolve out of the mere independent activity of

European humanity even in its totality. A special impulse had to be given towards the development of the Spiritual Soul itself.

And so, beginning in the time which I have now described, we witness the rise of two spiritual streams. The one was represented by the quasi-Arabian philosophers who, working from the West of Europe, influenced European civilisation very strongly—far more so than is commonly supposed. The other was the stream which fought against the former one with the utmost intensity and severity, representing it to Europe as the most heretical of all.

For a long time after, this conflict was felt with great intensity. You may still feel this if you consider the pictures in which Dominican Monks, or St. Thomas Aquinas alone, are represented in triumph—that is to say, in the triumph of an altogether different conception which emphasised above all things the individual and personal being of man, and worked to the end that man might acquire his thoughts as his own property. In these pictures we see the Dominicans portrayed, treading the representatives of Arabism under foot. The Arabians are there under their feet—they are being trodden underfoot.

The two streams were felt in this keen contrast for a long time after. An energy of feeling such as is contained in these pictures no longer exists in the humanity of to-day, which is rather apathetic. We need such energy of feeling very badly, not indeed for the things for which they battled, but for other things we need it.

Let us consider for a moment what they imagined. The in-breathing of thoughts as the cosmic ether from the Sublunary Sphere—that is the beginning of life. The holding of the breath—that is the earthly life itself. The out-breathing —that is the going-forth of the thoughts once more, but with an individually human colouring, into the cosmic ether, into the impulses of the sphere beneath the Moon, of the Sublunary Sphere.

What then is this out-breathing? It is the very same, my dear friends, of which we speak when we say: In the three days after death the etheric body of man expands. Man looks back upon his etheric body, slowly increasing in magnitude. He sees how his thoughts spread out into the cosmos. It is the very same, only it was then conceived—if I may say so—from a more subjective standpoint. It was indeed quite true, how these people felt and experienced it. They felt the cycle of life more deeply than it is felt to-day.

Nevertheless, if their idea had become dominant in Europe, only a feeble feeling of the Ego would have evolved in the men of European civilisation. The Spiritual Soul would not have been able to emerge; the Ego would not have grasped itself in the 'I think.' The idea of immortality would have become vaguer and vaguer. Men would increasingly have fixed their attention on that which lives and weaves in the far reaches of the Sublunary Sphere as a remnant of the human being who has lived here on this earth.

They would have felt the spirituality of the earth as its extended atmosphere. They would have felt themselves belonging to the earth, but not as individual men distinct from the earth. Through their feeling of "It thinks in me," the men whom I described above felt themselves intimately connected with the earth. They did not feel themselves as individualities in the same degree as the men of the rest of Europe were beginning to feel themselves, however indistinctly.

We must, however, also bear in mind the following. Only the spiritual stream of which I have just spoken, was aware of the fact that when man dies the thoughts he received during his earthly life are living and weaving in the cosmic ether that surrounds the earth. This idea was violently attacked by those other personalities who arose chiefly within the Dominican Order. They on their side declared that man is an individuality, and that we must concentrate above all on his individuality which passes through the gate of death, not on what is dissolved in the universal cosmic ether. This was emphasised paramountly, albeit not exclusively,—emphasised representatively, I would say, —by the Dominicans. They stood up sharply and vigorously for the idea of the individuality of man, as against the other stream which I characterised before. But precisely as a result of this a certain condition came about. For let us now consider these representatives—shall we say—of individualism.

After all, it was the individually coloured thoughts which passed into the universal ether. And those who fought against the former stream—just because they were still vividly aware that this was being said, that this idea existed, —were troubled and disquieted by what was *really* there.

This anxiety, notably among the greatest thinkers,—this anxiety as a result of the forces expanding and dissolving and passing on the human thoughts to the cosmic ether,—did not really come to an end until the 16th or 17th century.

We must somehow be able to transplant ourselves into the inner life of soul of these people,—those especially who belonged to the Dominican Order. Only then do we gain an idea, how much they were disquieted by what was really left as an heritage from the dead,—which they, with their conception, no longer could nor dared believe in.

We must transplant ourselves into the hearts and minds of these people. No great man of the 13th or 14th century could have thought so drily, so abstractly or in such cold and icy concepts as the men of to-day. When the men of to-day are standing up for any ideas or theories, it seems as though it were a recognised condition for so doing that one's heart should first be torn out of one's body. At that time it was not so. At that time there was deep feeling, there was *heartiness* in all that men upheld as their ideas. But in a case such as I am now citing, this heartiness also involved the presence of an intense inner conflict.

That philosophy, for instance, which proceeded from the Dominican Order was evolved under the most appalling inner conflicts. I mean that philosophy which afterwards had such a strong influence on life—for life at that time was still far more dependent on the authority of individual men.

There was no such popular education at that time. All culture and education—all that the people knew—eventually merged into the possession of a few. And as a consequence, these few reached up far more to a real philosophic life and striving. And in all that then flowed out into civilisation, these inner conflicts which they lived through, were contained.

To-day one reads the works of the Schoolmen and is conscious only of the driest thoughts. But it is the readers of to-day who are dry. Those who wrote these works were by no means dry in heart or mind. They were filled with inner fire in relation to their thoughts. Moreover, this inner fire was due to the striving to hold at bay the objective influence of thoughts.

When a man of to-day thinks on philosophic questions or questions of world-outlook, nothing is there, so to speak, to worry him. A man of to-day can think the greatest nonsense—he thinks it in perfect calm and peace of mind. Humanity has already evolved for so long within the Spiritual Soul, that no such disquieting occurs, as would occur, for instance, if individuals among us felt how the thoughts of men appear when they flow out after death into the ethereal environment of the earth. To-day, such things as could still be experienced in the 13th or 14th century, are quite unknown. Then it would happen that a younger priest would come to an older priest, telling of the inner tortures which he was undergoing in remaining true to his religious faith, and expressing it in this wise: 'I am pursued by the spectres of the dead.'

Speaking of the spectres of the dead, they meant precisely what I have just described. That was a time when men could still grow deeply into what they learned. In such a community—a Dominican community for instance,—they learned that man is individual and has his own individual immortality. They learned that it is a false and heretical idea to conceive, with respect to Thought, a kind of universal soul comprising all the earth. They learned to attack this heresy with all their might. And yet, in certain moments when they took deep counsel with themselves, they would feel the objective and influential presence of the thoughts which were left behind as relics by the dead. Then they would say to themselves, 'Is it quite right for me to be doing what I am doing? Here is something intangible, working into my soul. I cannot rise against it—I am held fast by it.'

The intellects of the men of that time,—of many of them at any rate,—were still so constituted that they were quite generally aware of the speaking of the dead, at least for some days after death. And when the one had ceased to speak, another would begin. With respect to such things too, they felt themselves immersed in the all-pervading spiritual —or at the very least, ethereal—essence of the universe.

Coming down into our own time, this living feeling with the Universal All has ceased. In return for it we have achieved the conscious life in the Spiritual Soul, while all the spiritual reality that surrounds us (surrounds us as a reality, no less so than tables or chairs, trees or rivers) works only upon the depths of our subconsciousness. The inwardness of life, the spiritual inwardness, has passed away. It must first be acquired again by spiritual-scientific knowledge livingly received.

We must think livingly upon the knowledge of spiritual science, and we shall do so if we dwell upon such facts of life as lie by no means very far behind us. Imagine a Scholastic thinker or writer of the 13th century. He writes down his thoughts. Nowadays it is easy work to think, for men have grown accustomed to think intellectualistically. At that time it was only at the beginning, and was still difficult. Man was still conscious of a tremendous inner effort. He was conscious of fatigue in thinking even as in hewing wood, if I may use the trivial comparison. To-day the thinking of many men has become quite automatic. We of to-day are scarcely overcome by the longing to follow up every one of our thoughts with our own human personality! We hear a man of to-day letting one thought arise out of another like an automaton. We cannot follow, we do not know why, for there is no inner necessity in it. And yet so long as a man is living in the body he should follow up his thoughts with his own personality. Afterwards they will soon take a different course; they will spread out and expand, when he is dead.

So could a man be sitting there at that time, defending with every weapon of sharp incisive thought the doctrine of individual man, so as to save the doctrine of individual immortality. So could he be rising in polemics against Averroes, or others of that stream of thought which I described at the beginning of this lecture. But there was another possibility. For especially in the case of an outstanding man like Averroes, that which proceeded from him, dissolving after his death like a kind of spectre in the Sublunary Sphere, might well be gathered up again by the Moon itself at the end of that Sphere, and remain behind. Having enlarged and expanded, it might even be reduced again, and shape and form be given to it, till it was consolidated once again into a being built, if I may say so, in the ether. That could well happen. Then would a man be sitting there, trying to lay the foundations of individualism, carrying on his polemic against Averroes; and Averroes would appear before him as a threatening figure, disturbing, putting off his mind.

The most important of the Scholastic writings which arose in the 13th century were directed against Averroes who was long dead. They made polemics against the man long dead, against the doctrine which he had left behind. Then he arose to prove to them that his thoughts had become condensed, consolidated once again and thus were living on.

There were indeed these inner conflicts, before the beginning of the new age of consciousness. And they were such that we to-day should see once more their full intensity and depth and inwardness. Words after all are words. The men of later times can but receive what lies behind the words, with such ideas as they possess. But within the words there were often rich contents of inner life. They pointed to a life of soul such as I have now described.

These, then, are the two streams, and they have remained active, fundamentally speaking, to this day. The one—albeit now only working from the spiritual world, yet all the stronger there,—would fain impress it upon man that a universal life of thoughts surrounds the earth, and that in thoughts man breathes-in soul and spirit. The other stream desires above all to point out that man should make himself independent of such universality. The former stream is more like a vague intangible presence in the spiritual environment of the earth, perceptible to-day to many men (for there are still such men) when in peculiar nights they lie there on their beds and listen to the void, and out of the void all manner of doubts are born in them as to what they are asserting to-day so definitely and so surely in their own individuality.

Meanwhile in other folk, who always sleep soundly because they are so well satisfied with themselves, we have the unswerving emphasis on the individual principle.

This battle, after all, is smouldering still at the very foundations of European culture. It is there to this day; and in the things that are taking place outwardly at the surface of our life, we have after all scarcely anything else than the beating of the surface-waves from that which is still present in the depths of souls,—a relic of the deeper and intenser inner life of yonder time.

Many souls of that time are here again in present earthly life. In a certain way they have conquered what then disquieted them so much in their surface consciousness—disquieted them at least in certain moments of their surface consciousness.

But in the depths it smoulders all the more, in many minds and hearts to-day. Spiritual science, once again, is here to draw attention also to such historic facts as these.

But we must not forget the following. In the same measure in which men become unconscious, during earthly life, of what is there none the less, namely the thoughts in the ether in the immediate environment of the earth—in the same measure, therefore, in which they acquire the 'I think' as their own possession—their human soul is narrowed down. Man passes through the gate of death with a contracted soul.

The narrowed soul has carried untrue, imperfect, inconsistent earthly thoughts into the cosmic ether, and these work back again upon the minds of men. Thence there arise such social movements as we see arise to-day. We must understand these too as to their inner origin. Then we shall recognise that there is no other cure, no other healing for these social ideas, destructive as they often are, than the spreading of the truth about the spiritual life and being.

Call to mind the lectures we have given here, especially the historic ones taking into account the idea of reincarnation and leading to so many definite examples. These lectures will have shown you how things work beneath the surface of external history. You will have seen how that which lives in one historic age is carried over into a later one by men returning into earthly life. But everything spiritual plays its part, between death and a new birth, in moulding what is carried by man from one earth-life into another.

To-day it would be good if many souls would attain for themselves that objectivity to which we can address ourselves, awakening an inner understanding, when we describe the men who lived in the twilight of the Intellectual or Mind-Soul age.

Some of the men who lived at that time are here again to-day. Deep in their souls they underwent the evening twilight of an age, and through the constant attacks they suffered from the spectres of which I have now spoken, they have, after all, absorbed deep doubts as to the unique validity of what is intellectualistic.

This doubt can well be understood. For about the 13th century there were many men—men of knowledge, who stood in the midst of the life of learning, almost entirely theological as it then was—men for whom it was a deep conscience question: What will now become?

Such souls had often carried with them into that time

mighty contents from their former incarnations. They gave it an intellectualistic colouring; but they felt this all as a declining stream. While at the rising stream—pressing forward as it was to individuality—they felt the pangs of conscience. Until at length those philosophers arose who stood under an influence which has really killed all meaning. To speak radically, we will say: those who stood under the influence of Descartes! For many, even among those who had their place in the Scholasticism of an earlier time, had already fallen into the Cartesian way of thought. I do not say that they became philosophers. These things underwent many a change. When men begin to think along these lines the strangest nonsense becomes self-understood. To Descartes, as you know, is due the saying 'I think, therefore I am.'

Countless clever thinkers have accepted this as true: 'I think, therefore I am.' Yet the result is this: From morning until evening I think, therefore I am. Then I fall asleep. I do not think, therefore I am not. I wake up again, I think, therefore I am. I fall asleep, and as I now do not think, I am not. This then is the consequence: A man not only falls asleep, but ceases to be when he falls asleep. There is no less fitting proof of the existence of the spirit of man than the theorem: 'I think.' Yet this began to be the most widely accepted statement in the age of evolution of Consciousness (the age of the Spiritual Soul). When we point to such things to-day, it is like a sacrilege—we cannot help ourselves!

But over against all this, I would now tell you of a kind of conversation. Though it is not historically recorded, by spiritual research it can be discovered among the real facts that happened. It was a conversation that took place between an older and a younger Dominican, somewhat as follows:—

The younger man said, 'Thinking takes hold of men. Thought, the shadow of reality, takes hold of them. In ancient times, thought was always the last revelation of the living Spirit from above. But now, thought is the very thing that has forgotten that living Spirit. Now it is experienced as a mere shadow. Verily, when a man sees a shadow, he knows the shadow points to some reality. The realities are there indeed. Thinking itself is not to be attacked, but only the fact that we have lost the living Spirit from our thinking.'

The older man replied, 'In Thinking, through the very fact that man is turning his attention with loving interest to outer Nature, (while he accepts Revelation as Revelation and does not seek to approach it with his thinking),—in Thinking, to compensate for the former heavenly reality, an earthly reality must be found once more.'

'What will happen?' said the younger man. 'Will European humanity be strong enough to find this earthly reality of thought, or will it only be weak enough to lose the heavenly reality?'

This dialogue truly contains all that can still hold good with regard to European civilisation. For after the intermediate time, with the darkening of the living quality of thought, mankind must now attain the living thought once more. Otherwise humanity will remain weak, and with the reality of thought will lose its own reality. Therefore it is most necessary, since the entry of our Christmas impulse, that we in the Anthroposophical Movement speak without reserve in forms of living thought. For otherwise it will come about, more and more, that even the things we know from this source or from that—as for instance, that man has a physical body, an etheric body and an astral body,—will only be taken hold of with the forms of dead thinking.

These things must not be taken hold of with the forms of dead thinking. For then they become distorted, misrepresented truth, and not the truth itself.

So much I wanted to describe to-day. We must attain a living, sympathetic interest, a longing to go beyond the ordinary history and to attain that history which must and can be read in the living Spirit, which history shall more and more be cultivated in the Anthroposophical Movement. To-day, my dear friends, I wished to place before your souls, as it were, the concrete outline of our programme in this direction.

Much has been said to-day in aphorism. The inner connection will dawn upon you if you attempt, not so much to follow up with intellect, but to feel with your whole being, what was desired to be said to-day. You must attempt to feel it knowingly, to know it feelingly, in order that not only what is said but what is heard within our circles may be sustained more and more by real spirituality.

We need education to spiritual hearing, spiritual listening. Only then shall we develop the true spirituality among us. I wanted to awaken this feeling in you to-day; not so much to hold a systematic lecture, but to speak to your hearts, albeit calling to witness, as I did so, many a concrete spiritual fact.

II

Forces of Karmic Preparation in the Cosmos

To-day I shall have to say some more of how the karmic forces of preparation undergo their further course of evolution when man has passed through the gate of death. So far as the ordinary consciousness is concerned, the forming of karma, and indeed that whole intercourse with the world which we call 'karmic,' takes place in the human being in a more instinctive way. We see the animals act 'instinctively.' Words like 'instinct,' which are used so frequently in science and every-day life, are generally applied in a vague and undefined way. People make no real effort to associate them with clear conceptions. What is it that we call instinct in the animals? We know that the animals have a Group-soul. The animal, such as it is, is not a self-contained being. The Group-soul is standing there behind it. Now to what world does the Group-soul belong? We must first answer this question: Where do we find the Group-souls of the animals? They are certainly not to be found here in the physical world of sense. Here we have only the single individual animals. We do not find the Group-souls of the animals until, by Initiation or in the ordinary course of human evolution between death and a new birth, we come into that altogether different world which man passes through between his successive earthly lives. There indeed we find, among the beings with whom we are then together, including above all those of whom I have been speaking to you, those with whom we elaborate our karma, —there we find the Group-souls of the animals. And the animals that are here on the earth, when they act instinctively, they act out of the full consciousness of the Group-souls.

You may conceive it thus, my dear friends. (Dr. Steiner here made a drawing on the blackboard). Here we have the realm in which we live between death and a new birth; and out of it there work the forces which proceed from the Group-souls of the animals. And here upon this earth we have the single animals which act and move about, guided as it were by threads which pass to the Group-souls—the beings whom we ourselves discover in the realm between death and a new birth. Such in truth is instinct.

It is obvious that a materialistic world-conception cannot explain instinct, for instinct is:—to act out of that sphere of being which you will find described as Spirit-land in my *Theosophy* for example, and in my *Occult Science*.

For man however it is different. Man too has instinct, but when he acts through his instinct, he is not acting out of yonder Spirit-realm, but out of his own former lives on earth. He is acting across time, out of his former earthly lives, out of a whole number of former lives on earth.

As the spiritual realm works upon the animals, causing them to act instinctively, so do the former incarnations of man work on his later incarnations in such a way that he instinctively lives out his karma. But this is a spiritual instinct—an instinct that works within the Ego.

It is just by understanding this, that we shall come to understand the absolute consistency of this instinctive working with human freedom. For the freedom of man proceeds from the very realm out of which the animals act instinctively, namely the realm of the spirit.

To-day we will concern ourselves especially with the way in which this instinct is gradually prepared when man passes through the gate of death. Here in earthly life, as we have seen, the inner experience of karma is instinctive. It takes its course beneath the surface of consciousness; but the moment we pass through the gate of death we become objectively conscious, during the first few days, of all the experiences which we first underwent on earth. We have them before us in ever expanding pictures; and what we thus behold as a great tableau of our life contains, in addition, all that took place instinctively in the working of our karma.

When man passes through the gate of death, and his life, expanding ever more and more, is unfolded before his eyes, there goes with it all that was instinctive, of which he was not conscious in his life—the web of karma. He does not actually see it in the first days after death. But what he would otherwise perceive only in pale images of memory, this he now beholds vividly as a living configuration, nor does he fail to perceive that something more is contained in it than ordinary memory. And if we look with the vision of Initiation on all that the human being has before him at this stage, we can describe it as follows:

The man himself, who has passed through the gate of death having possessed the ordinary consciousness during his earthly life, sees his life spread out before him as a mighty panorama. But he sees it only 'from in front.' The vision of Initiation sees it also from the other side—'from behind,' as it were. The human being himself sees it only from the one side. With the vision of the Initiate we can see it 'from behind,' and then the whole web of karmic relationships springs forth from it. We behold this web of karmic relationships arising to begin with from the Thoughts, that lived within the Will during the man's earthly life. But immediately something else enters into it, my dear friends.

I have often emphasised the fact:—The thoughts we experience *consciously* during our earthly life are dead thoughts. But the thoughts that are woven into our karma, the thoughts that now emerge, are *living*. Thus—on the 'other side,' as it were, of the panorama of our life—the living thoughts spring forth. And now, (this is a fact of untold significance)—now the Beings of the Third Hierarchy draw near, and receive what is springing forth from the 'other side' of the panorama. Angels, Archangels and Archai draw it into themselves, they breathe it in!

This takes place during the time when man ascends on his way upward, after death, to the end of the Moon Sphere.

Thereafter he enters the Moon Sphere, and his backward journey through his life begins, lasting—as we know—a third of the time he spent on earth, or—to speak more accurately—lasting for the same length of time as the periods of sleep which he spent while he was on the earth.

I have often described how this backward journey through life takes place. We may now ask ourselves: What is man's condition in ordinary sleep, in relation to the condition in which he finds himself directly after death? Normally when he goes to sleep, man as a being of soul and spirit is only in his astral body and his Ego. He has not his etheric body with him, for this has remained behind in the bed. Hence his thoughts remain unliving; they have no active power, they are mere pictures. But when he passes through the gate of death, to begin with he takes his etheric body with him, and the etheric body begins to expand. Now the etheric body has a life-giving quality, not only for the physical existence, but for the thoughts themselves. By this means the thoughts can become alive, inasmuch as man has taken his etheric body with him. The etheric body, as it frees itself, carries forth the living thoughts from man to the Angels, Archangels and Archai, who in their Divine Grace receive the thoughts.

This, if I may so describe it, is the first Act that is unfolded in the life between death and a new birth. Beyond the threshold of death, the Beings of the Third Hierarchy approach that which loosens itself from the human being —which is entrusted to his etheric body as it dissolves away. The Beings of the Third Hierarchy receive it into Their care. And we as human beings on the earth utter a simple and good, a wonderful and beautiful prayer, when we think of the connection of life and death, or of one who has passed through the gate of death, in this way, saying:—

Angels, Archangels and Archai in the Ether-weaving
receive the human being's Web of Destiny.

For as we say these words we turn our eyes to a real spiritual fact. Much depends upon it, whether human beings on the earth *think* the spiritual facts or not: whether they merely accompany the Dead with thoughts that remain behind on the earth, or accompany them on their further path with thoughts which are a true image of what takes place in yonder realm which they have entered.

This, my dear friends, appears so infinitely desirable to Initiate Science:—That thoughts shall be within the earthly life, which are a true image of real spiritual happenings. By merely thinking in theories—enumerating so many higher members of the human being, and the like,—we achieve no union with the spiritual world. We can only do so by thinking the realities that are enacted there.

Therefore, human hearts should be ready to hear once more, what human hearts *did* hear in the old ages of Initiation, in the ancient Mysteries, when they called out impressively, again and again, to those who were about to be initiated:—'Accompany the Dead in their further Destinies!' 'Memento mori' is all that is left of it now, a more or less abstract exhortation which no longer affects the human being deeply. For it no longer expands his consciousness into a life more living than this life in the world of the senses.

Now the reception of the human web of destiny by Angels, Archangels and Archai, unfolds before us in this wise:—we have the impression: it lives and moves and has its being in the bluish-violet ethereal atmosphere. It is a living and weaving in the bluish-violet atmosphere of the ether.

When the etheric body is dissolved, that is, when the thoughts have been breathed-in by the Angels, Archangels and Archai, then, after a few days, man enters into that backward course of life which I have described to you. There he experiences his deeds, his impulses of will, his tendencies of thought, in the way in which they worked on other men, to whom he did either good or evil. He enters right into the minds and feelings of other men. He does not live in his own mind. With the clear consciousness that it is *his* concern, he undergoes all that took place in the depths of other human beings' souls, with whom he entered into any kind of karmic relationship,—to whom he did anything whatever good or ill. And once again it shows itself, how that which the human being thus experiences is *received.* He experiences it in fullness of reality—a reality, which I had to describe not long ago as a reality more real than that of the senses between birth and death. He experiences a reality in the midst of which he stands more fully, more glowingly than in any reality of this earthly life down here.

But if we look at it once more with the vision and insight of Initiation from the ' other side,' we see all this, which the human being experiences, *received* into the essence, into the reality and being of the Kyriotetes, Dynamis and Exusiai. They draw into themselves, as it were, the ' Negative ' of the human deeds. This wondrous process unfolds before the vision of the Initiate. The consequences of man's actions, transformed in righteousness and justice, are taken up into the Exusiai, Dynamis and Kyriotetes.

Now the vision of all this transplants him who has it into such a consciousness that he knows himself to be in the centre of the Sun and with it of the whole Planetary system. From the aspect of the Sun he beholds what is now taking place. He sees a lilac-coloured living and weaving; he sees the Exusiai, Dynamis and Kyriotetes absorbing the human deeds, transformed into righteousness, in the living and weaving of a pale violet, lilac-coloured astral atmosphere.

Here, you see, we have the truth:—the aspect of the Sun as it appears to earthly man is only the one side, it is seen here from the periphery. From the centre the Sun is seen as the field of action for the living spiritual deeds of Exusiai, Dynamis and Kyriotetes. There it is all spiritual action, spiritual happening. There we find as it were the ' other side ' of the pictures of that earthly life which we experienced consciously here between birth and death.

Once again we can think truly of what is happening there. We must think of the word ' *verwesen* ' which is ordinarily used for the fading, dying, destroying process, the passing out of existence,—in its true and original meaning, which is: ' to carry the real Being away.' (As when we say ' to forgive ' or ' to forego,' which means in reality a ' giving away ' in devotion).

Thinking thus we may say:—

In Exusiai, Dynamis and Kyriotetes, in the astral feeling of the Cosmos the righteous consequences of the earthly life of man die into the realm of Being.

At length, this too has been accomplished. Man after death has lived through a third of the time of his earthly life. Journeying backward, he feels himself once more at the starting point of his earthly life—in the spaces of the Spirit—at the moment before his entry into his past earthly life. And now, we may say, he enters through the centre of the Sun into the essential Spirit-land, and in the Spirit-land his earthly deeds—transformed into the Divine Righteousness—are received into the activity of the first Hierarchy. They come into the domain of Seraphim, Cherubim and Thrones. Man feels, as he steps out into this new kingdom:—'All that took place through me on earth is now being received by Seraphim, Cherubim and Thrones, into their own active Being.'

Consider well what this means, my dear friends. We are thinking truly of what happens to the Dead in his further life after death, if we cherish the thought: The web of destiny which he wove here on earth, is caught up, to begin with, by the Angels, Archangels and Archai. In the next part of the life between death and new birth, They bear it into the kingdom of Exusiai, Dynamis and Kyriotetes. These in turn are gathered in and woven around by the Beings of the first Hierarchy. And in the process, ever and again, man's action upon earth is received into the Being—into the Deeds of Being, into the living Action—of Thrones and Cherubim and Seraphim.

Once again we are thinking rightly if to the first and the second saying we now add the third, which is as follows:—

In Thrones and Cherubim and Seraphim, as their Deeds of Being, the justly transmuted 'fruits of the earthly life' of man are resurrected.

Thus we can turn the gaze of Initiation upon what is going on perpetually in the spiritual world. Here on earth we have the unfolding life and action of men with their instinct of karma, their ceaseless weaving of destiny—a weaving more or less similar to the weaving of thought. Looking up into the spiritual worlds, we see there what were once the earthly deeds of man—having passed through Angeloi, Archangeloi, Archai, Exusiai, Dynamis and Kyriotetes—received by the Thrones and Cherubim and Seraphim, expanding as their heavenly Deeds above.

1. *Es empfangen Angeloi, Archangeloi, Archai im Aetherweben das Schicksalsnetz des betreffenden Menschen.*
   Angels, Archangels and Archai in the Ether-weaving receive his Web of Destiny.
2. *Es verwesen in Exusiai, Dynamis, Kyriotetes—im Astralempfinden des Kosmos—die gerechten Folgen des Erdenlebens des Menschen.*
   In Exusiai, Dynamis, Kyriotetes, in the astral feeling of the Cosmos, the righteous consequences of his earthly life die into the realm of Being.
3. *Es auferstehen in Thronen, Cherubim, Seraphim—als deren Tatenwesen—die gerechten Ausgestaltungen des Erdenlebens des Menschen.*
   In Thrones, Cherubim and Seraphim, as their Deeds of Being, the justly transmuted fruits of his earthly life are resurrected.

This is a succession of spiritual facts infinitely sublime and significant especially for our present age. For the dominion of Michael has now begun, and in this world-historic moment it is as though we could behold the deeds of those who lived upon earth before the end of Kali-Yuga, in the 1880's and 90's. That which was then enacted among men on earth, has now been received by Thrones, Cherubim and Seraphim. Yet never was the spiritual contrast-of-light so great as it is to-day, in the realm of these spiritual facts.

In the 1880's one could look upward and see how the people of the Revolution period of the middle of the 19th century, were received as to their deeds by Thrones and Cherubim and Seraphim. But as one looked, a kind of darkling cloud settled over the middle of the 19th century. What one then saw passing into the realm of Seraphim, Cherubim and Thrones, lighted up only a very little.

But to-day, when we look back to all that took place at the end of the 19th century—the deeds of men, their relations to one another,—having seen it clearly still, only a short time ago, it vanishes away . . . We saw it clearly still, a moment since,—all that took place in that declining age of Kali-Yuga,—like thought-masses wafted away before our eyes . . . We saw what was worked out in destiny among the human beings of the end of Kali-Yuga. And then it vanishes, and we behold in clear, radiant light what became of it as it passed heavenward.

This fact bears witness to the immense importance of what is taking place at the present time in the transmutation of the earthly deeds of men into the heavenly deeds of souls.

What man experiences as his destiny or karma takes place for him, within him and about him, from earthly life to earthly life. But in the heavenly worlds the consequences of what he did and experienced on earth go working on—and they work on even into the historic shaping of this earthly life. For there are many things which are not grasped or controlled by the individual human being here upon earth.

My dear friends, you must take this statement in its full weight and importance. The individual man experiences his destiny. But as soon as two human beings are working together, something more arises,—*more* than the working out of the individual destinies of the one and of the other. Something takes place as between the two, transcending the individual experiences of either. Ordinary consciousness perceives no connection of what happens between man and man, with what goes on in the spiritual worlds above. For ordinary consciousness the connection is at most established when sacred spiritual actions are brought into this physical world of sense,—as when in sacred cult or ritual men consciously transform their physical actions so as to make them actions of the spiritual world at the same time.

But in a far wider sphere, all that happens between man and man is *more* than what the individual man experiences as his destiny. All that is not merely the destiny of individual men, but that is brought about by the feeling-together and working-together of men on earth, is for ever in connection with the deeds of Seraphim and Cherubim and Thrones above. Into the latter there flow the deeds of men in their mutual connection with one another, as well as the individual earthly lives of men.

Most important at this point is the wider range of vision that opens out for the Initiate. For to-day as we look upward we behold the heavenly deeds and consequences of what took place on earth in the late 70's, the 80's and 90's of last century. And it is as though a fine spiritual rain were falling, falling to the earth, moistening the souls of men, impelling them to many things that arise historically in our time, in the relations between man and man.

Once more we can see, how there lives again to-day in living mirror-images of thought—through Seraphim, Cherubim and Thrones,—what was enacted here on earth by men of the 1870's, 80's and 90's.

When one sees through these things, again and again one must say to oneself: —Here you are speaking to a human being of to-day. What he says to you out of the commonly accepted opinion—not from his own emotions or inner impulses but simply as a person of this age—seems often as though it stood in connection with human beings who lived in the 70's, 80's and 90's of last century. It is so really. We see many a human being of to-day as though he were in a meeting of departed spirits, surrounded by human beings who are busily at work upon him. But in reality they are only the after-images, rained down from heaven, of what lived through human beings upon earth in the last third of the 19th century.

Thus in a spiritual sense the shades—the real ghosts, I would say,—of a former age are roaming about in a later age. This is one of the more intimate workings of karma which are indeed widely present in the world, though they frequently remain unnoticed even by the most occult of occultists. To many a man of to-day, when he utters some opinion not individual but stereotyped, one would fain whisper in his ear: 'That was said to you by this man or that, of the last third of the 19th century.'

Only so does life become a real totality. And in this respect once more we must say of the present age—the age that began with the end of the Kali-Yuga—that it is different from all historic ages preceding it. It is different in this sense, that in very truth the human deeds on earth in the last third of the 19th century have the greatest imaginable influence on the first third of the 20th.

My dear friends, I am saying something far removed from any superstitious use of words. I say it with the full consciousness of voicing an exact and scientific fact:—Never before did the ghosts of the preceding age move about among men so palpably as they do in *this* present time. And if men fail to perceive them, it is not because we are living in an age of darkness. Rather is it that they are still dazzled by the light of the new Age of Light. But as a consequence, what is done among us by the shades of the past century is an all the more fruitful field for the people of Ahriman. Though man is unaware of it, the people of Ahriman are working to-day in a more than usually evil way. They are at pains—if I may so describe it—to galvanize into Ahrimanic life as many as possible of these ghosts of the past century and bring them to bear upon the human beings of to-day. This Ahrimanic quality of our age is fostered most of all when societies are formed to popularise erroneous ideas of the 19th century—ideas which, for all men of insight, are out of date and discarded. There never was a time when amateurish persons popularised the outlived errors of the past to the extent they do to-day. Indeed we have opportunities on all hands to-day, to acquaint ourselves with the essential nature of the deeds of Ahriman. We need only visit many a meeting where people are working out of the ordinary consciousness. We have many an opprtunity to learn to know the Ahrimanism in the world to-day, for it is at work most strongly. By the very path which I have now described, it hinders people from receiving into their hearts and souls what must come forth *anew*, what was not there before,—what is coming to the light of day in Anthroposophy.

How happy men are when they can somehow contrive to cover up the *New*, that is coming forth in Anthroposophy to-day, with some *old* saying. How contented they are, if in some lecture that I give something occurs of which they can subsequently prove: 'Look, here it is in an old book!' In reality, of course, it is there in quite a different form, coming out of altogether different foundations of consciousness. The people of to-day have so little courage to receive what grows on the soil of the living present. Their minds are set at rest as soon as they can bring something forward out of the past.

It shows, my dear friends, how powerfully the impulses of the past work upon the men of the present time,—how contented they feel under these influences. It is due to the fact that the 19th century is working still so strongly into the 20th. Future historians—who will write their descriptions spiritually, as we write ours to-day by reference to outer documents,—future historians will have to describe this feature above all, and they may well express it in some such words as these:—'Look at the first three decades of the 20th century. Nearly everything appears as though it were being done by the shades, the images of deeds of men of the end of the 19th century.'

At this point I may perhaps say a word that is truly not intended in any political sense. Politics must be eliminated altogether from our Society. May I say this word, my dear friends, simply as a characterisation of the facts:—We can look back on the stupendous, revolutionising actions—or rather, happenings, I should have said, for they were no really active deeds,—which took place notably in the second decade of the 20th century. It has been said so often that it has become a truism. Since time has been, since men have written history, such world-shaking events have not happened.

But are not men standing in the midst of them as though they were not there at all? We see it everywhere,—it is as though the revolutionising events were taking place outside the human beings, and the latter had no part in them at all. Almost every man we meet to-day, we would fain ask of him: ' Did you really *live* through the second decade of this century? ' And how much more do we feel it when we look at it from a somewhat different point of view! How helpless, how infinitely helpless do the human beings seem to-day—helpless in judgment, helpless in action. Never were there such difficulties as there are to-day in filling the ministerial benches—the Cabinets! Consider only how curious this is, —how helpless men are in the midst of the events. At long last we are impelled to raise the question, who then *is* doing anything? Who is playing an active part? My dear friends, more than any of the men of the present time, it is the men of the last third of the 19th century! Their shadow-forces are to be seen at work in everything.

This is the very secret of our time. Never were the Dead so powerful as are the Dead of the last third of the 19th century. This too is a world-aspect of realities.

When we enter into the spiritual content of these things in a single instance, we often come to strange conclusions. I recently had to consider whether I would alter this or that in the new edition of my books, written in the 70's, 80's and 90's of last century. The pedants of to-day declare: Everything has altered, the scientific theories and hypotheses of that time are out-of-date and long ago discarded. But when we look at it from a standpoint of reality, we can alter nothing at all! For in reality, behind everyone who writes a book to-day, or lectures from a professional chair, there stands the shade, the shadow-picture of another. There they still are,—the Du Bois Reymonds, the Helmholtzes, the Haeckels,—all those who were the spokesmen of that time, (in medicine the Obholzers, the Billroths and the rest) —they are still speaking.

Here we are lifting a corner of the veil, a secret of the present time. Initiate Science says in all truth: 'Never were the Dead so mighty as in our age!'

This is what I wish to insert to-day in the course of our studies on karma.

III

The Spiritual Foundations of Anthroposophical Endeavour

We have seen how the study of karma, wherein the destiny of man is contained, leads us from the affairs of the farthest universe—from the worlds of the stars—down to the tenderest experiences of the human heart, inasmuch as the heart is an expression of all that man feels working upon him during life,—of all that happens to him in the whole nexus of earth-existence. When we try to arrive at our judgments through a deeper understanding of the karmic connections, we are driven again and again to look into these two domains of world-existence which lie so far removed from one another. Indeed we must say: Whatever else we may be studying,—be it Nature, or the more natural configuration of human evolution in history or in the life of nations—none of these leads us so high up into cosmic realms as the study of karma. The study of karma makes us altogether aware of the connections between human life here upon earth and that which goes on in the wide universe. We see this human life taking its course on earth, unfolding till about the 70th year of life, when in a certain connection it attains its limit. Whatever lies beyond this is in reality a life given by grace. What lies below this limit stands under karmic influences, and these we shall now have to study.

It is possible, as I have often mentioned from varied points of view, to put the length of human life on earth at about 72 years. Now 72 years, seen in relation to the secrets of the cosmos, is a remarkable number, the true significance of which only begins to dawn upon us when we consider what I may call the cosmic secret of human earthly life.

We have already described what the world of the stars is from a spiritual point of view. When we enter on a new earthly life, we return, so to speak, from the world of stars to this life on earth.

At this point once more it is astonishing how the ancient ideas—even if we do not take our start from tradition—simply emerge again of their own accord when we approach these domains of life with the help of modern spiritual science. We have seen how the various planetary stars and fixed stars take part in human life and in all that permeates this human life on earth. If we have before us an earthly life that has taken its full course,—one that does not come to an end all too soon, but that has passed through half at least of the allotted earthly time,—then in the last resort we find this truth once more: The human being, inasmuch as he comes down from cosmic spiritual spaces into an earthly life, comes always from a certain star. We can trace the very direction of it, and it is not unreal—on the contrary, it is most exact, to say:—'The human being has his star.' If we take what is experienced beyond all space and time between death and a new birth, and translate this into its spatial image, we can say: Every man has his star, which determines what he has attained between death and a new birth.

He comes from the direction of a certain star. We may indeed receive into our minds this conception. The whole human race inhabiting the earth is to be found on the one hand by looking round about us upon earth, passing through these many continents, finding them peopled by the human beings who are now incarnated. And the others who are not on the earth, where in the universe shall we find them? Whither must we look in the great universe if we would turn our soul's gaze to them,—assuming that a certain time has elapsed since they went through the gate of death? The answer is: We look in the true direction when we look out upon the starry heavens. There are the souls—or at least the directions which will enable us to find the souls—who are spending their life between death and a new birth.

We see and comprehend the entire human race that inhabits the earth, when we look upward and downward.

Those alone who are now on the way thither or returning thence, we find in the planetary region. But we can certainly not speak of the midnight hour of existence between death and a new birth, without thinking of some star which the human being as it were indwells between death and a new birth (albeit we must always bear in mind what I have said about the beings of the stars).

Then, my dear friends, we shall approach the cosmos with this knowledge. Away there are the stars, the cosmic signs from which there shines and lightens down upon us the soul-life of those who are between death and a new birth. And then we become aware that we can look also at the constellations of stars, saying to ourselves: ' How is all this, that we behold in cosmic spaces, connected with the life of man? ' We look up with a new fulness of heart and mind to the silvery moon, the dazzling blaze of the sun, the twinkling stars at night-time, and we feel ourselves united even humanly with all of these. This is what Anthroposophy is to attain at last for the souls of men: they shall feel themselves united even in a human way with the whole cosmos. It is at this point that certain secrets of cosmic existence first begin to dawn upon us.

The sun rises and sets; the stars rise and set. We can trace how the sun sets, for example in the region where there are certain groups of stars. We can trace what is now called the apparent course of the stars, circling round the earth. We can trace the course of the sun. In 24 hours, the sun circles around the earth—' apparently ' as we say nowadays,—and the stars too circle around the earth. So we say: but it is not *quite* correct. For if again and again we attentively observe the course of stars and sun, we perceive at length that the sun does not always rise at the same time in relation to the stars. It grows ever a little later. Day after day it arrives a little later at the place where it was on the previous day in relation to the stars. These spaces of time, by which the sun remains behind the stars in their course, add up till they become an hour, two hours, three hours, and at length a day. Thus at length the time approaches when we can say: The sun has remained behind the star by a whole day.

Now let us assume: Someone was born on the 1st of March in a particular year. And, let us say, he lived till the end of his 72nd year. He always celebrates his birthday on the 1st of March, for the sun says: His birthday is on the 1st of March. And he can celebrate it so, for throughout the 72 years of his life (though it progresses in relation to the stars) the sun shines forth ever and again in the neighbourhood of the star that shone when he came down to earth. But when he has lived for 72 years, a full day has elapsed. He has arrived at an age in life when the sun leaves the star into which it entered when he began his life. At his birthday now he is beyond the 1st of March. The star no longer says the same as the sun; the stars say it is the 2nd of March; the sun says it is the 1st. The human being has lost a cosmic day, for it takes just 72 years for the sun to remain behind a star.

During this time which the sun can spend in the region of his star, a man can live on earth. Then (under normal conditions) when the sun is no longer there to comfort his star for his life on earth, when the sun no longer says to his star: ' He is down there, and I from myself am giving thee what he—this human being—has to give to thee; and for the time being, as I cover thee, I am doing for him what thou dost for him between death and a new birth,' when the sun can no longer speak thus to the star, the star summons the man back again.

Thus you perceive the processes in the heavens immediately connected with human existence upon earth. In the mysteries of the heavens we see the age of man's life expressed. Man can live 72 years, because in this time the sun remains a day behind. After that time the sun can no longer comfort the star which it could comfort while it stood before and covered it. The star has become free again for the soul-spiritual work of man within the cosmos.

These things cannot be understood in any other way than

with reverence,—with that deep reverence which was called in the ancient Mysteries 'the reverence for that which is above.' For this reverence leads us ever and again to see what happens here on earth in connection with what is unfolded in the sublime, majestic writing of the stars. It is indeed a limited life men lead to-day, compared to what was still existing at the beginning of the 3rd Post-Atlantean epoch. They did not merely base their reckoning, their understanding of man, on that which describes his steps upon the earth; they reckoned with what the stars of the great universe are saying about the life of man.

Once we are attentive to such connections and able to receive them with reverence into our souls, then too we know: 'Whatever happens here on earth has its corresponding counterpart in the spiritual worlds.' In the writing of the stars is expressed the kind of connection that exists between what happens here, and what happened (to speak from the earthly point of view) 'some time ago' in the spiritual world. In truth our every reflection upon karma should be accompanied by holy reverence and awe before the secrets of the universe.

In such a mood of reverence, let us approach the studies of karma which we are to make here during the near future. To begin with let us take this fact: Here are sitting a number of human beings, a section of what we call the Anthroposophical Society; and though one of us may be united with this Anthroposophical Society by stronger links, and another by less strong, it is in all cases part of a man's destiny—and the destiny that underlies these things is powerful—it is a part of his destiny that he has found his way into the Anthroposophical Society. Moreover, it lies inherent in the spiritualisation which must come over the Anthroposophical Society since the Christmas Foundation Meeting:—We must become ever more conscious of the spiritual, cosmic realities that underlie such a community as this Society. For out of such a consciousness the individual will then be able to take his true stand in the Society. Hence you will understand—along with all the other responsibilities resulting from the Christmas Foundation Meeting—that we must now begin to say something too about the karma of the Anthroposophical Society. It is very complicated, for it is a karma of community,—a karma that arises from the karmic coming-together of many single human beings. Take in its true and deep meaning all that has been said in these lectures and all that results from the many relationships that have been unfolded here; then, my dear friends, you will yourselves perceive that what is taking place here in our midst—where a number of human beings are led by their karma into the Anthroposophical Society—has been preceded by many and important events which happened to these very human beings before they came down into this present earthly life—events moreover which were themselves the after-effects of what had taken place in former lives on earth.

Let your thought dwell for a moment on the great vistas that are opened up by such an idea as this. Then you will realise how this thought may by and by be deepened till there emerges the spiritual history that stands behind the Anthroposophical Society. But this cannot be accomplished all at once. It can only enter our consciousness slowly and gradually ; then only will it be possible to build even the conduct and action of the Anthroposophical Society on the foundations which are actually there for anthroposophists.

It is of course Anthroposophy as such which holds the Society together. In one way or another, everyone who finds his way into the Society must be seeking for Anthroposophy. And the preceding causes are to be sought for in the experiences which were undergone, by the souls who now become anthroposophists, before they came down into this earthly life.

At the same time, if we look out into the world with a clear perception of what has happened hitherto, we are also bound to admit: There are many human beings whom we find here or there in the world to-day, and of whom—looking at their connection with their pre-earthly life—we must say that they were truly pre-destined by their pre-natal life for the Anthroposophical Society; and yet, owing to certain other things, they are unable to find their way into it. There are far more of them than we generally think.

This must bring still nearer to our hearts the question: What is the pre-destination that leads a soul to Anthroposophy?

I will take my start from extreme examples, which are all the more instructive in shewing how the karmic forces work. In the Anthroposophical Society the question of karma does indeed arise before the individual in a more intensive way than in other realms of life. I need only say the following: The souls who are incarnated in a human body now,—to begin with we cannot possibly follow them back far enough to assume that they experienced directly in their past earthly lives anything that could lead them, for example, to Eurhythmy (to take this radical instance from within the Anthroposophical Movement). For Eurhythmy did not exist in the times when the souls who now seek for it were incarnated. Thus the burning question arises: How comes it that a soul finds its way into Eurhythmy out of the working of the karmic forces?

But so it is in all the domains of life. Souls are there to-day, seeking the way to that which Anthroposophy can give them. How do they come to unfold all the pre-dispositions of their karma from past earthly lives, precisely in this direction which leads them to Anthroposophy?

In the first place there are some souls who are driven to Anthroposophy with strong inner intensity. The intensity of these forces is not the same in all. Some souls are driven to Anthroposophy with such inward intensity that it seems as though they were steering straight towards it without any by-ways at all, finding their way directly into one domain or another of the anthroposophical life.

There are a number of souls who steer their cosmic way in this sense for the following reason: In past centuries, when they had their former life on earth, they felt with peculiar intensity that Christianity had reached a definite turning-point. They lived in an age when the main effect of Christianity was to pass over into a more or less instinctive human feeling. It was an age when Christianity was practised in a perfectly natural and simple way but quite instinctively; so that the question did not really occur to the souls of men: *Why* am I a Christian? Such souls we find especially if we turn our gaze to the 13th, 12th, 11th, 10th, 9th, and 8th centuries after Christ. There we find Christ-permeated souls, who were growing and evolving towards the age of Consciousness (the age of the Spiritual Soul), but who, since this age had not yet begun, were still receiving Christianity into the pure Mind-Soul. On the other hand, with respect to the worldly affairs of life, they already experienced the dawn of what the Spiritual Soul is destined to bring.

Thus their Christianity lived in a way unconsciously. It was in many respects a deeply pious Christianity, but it lived, if I may say so, leaving the head on one side and entering straight into the functions of the organism. Now that which is unconscious in one life becomes a degree more conscious in the next life on earth: and so this Christianity which had not become fully clear or self-conscious, became at length a challenge and a question for these human souls: '*Why* are we Christians?'

The outcome was (I am speaking in an introductory way to-day, hinting at matters which will be spoken of more fully afterwards) the outcome was that in the life between death and a new birth these souls had a certain connection once more in the spiritual world, especially in the first half of the 19th century. In the first half of the 19th century there were gatherings of souls in the spiritual world,—souls who took the consequences of the Christianity they had experienced on earth, finding it again in the radiance, in the all embracing glory of the spiritual world. Above all in the first half of the 19th century, there were souls in the life between death and a new birth who strove to translate into cosmic Imaginations what they had felt in a preceding Christian life on earth. The very thing that I once described here as a great cult or act of ritual was there enacted in the Supersensible. A large number of souls were gathered in these mutually-woven cosmic Imaginations, in these mighty pictures of a future existence, which they were to seek again in an altered form during their next life on earth.

But in all this was also interwoven all that had taken place between the 7th and 13th or 14th centuries A.D. by way of dire and painful inner conflicts, which were indeed more painful than is generally thought. For the souls to whom I now refer had undergone very much during that time; and all that they had thus undergone, they wove it into the mighty cosmic Imaginations which were woven together by a large number of souls in common, during the first half of the 19th century.

The great cosmic Imaginations that were thus woven were shot through on the one hand by something that I cannot otherwise describe than as a kind of longing and expectant feeling. Working out these mighty Imaginations, the souls experienced within them a concentrated feeling, gathered from manifold experiences, a concentrated feeling within their disembodied souls. It was a feeling which I can describe somewhat as follows: 'In our last life on earth we inclined towards the living experience of Christianity. Deeply we felt the Mysteries which tradition had preserved for all Christians, telling of the sacred and solemn happenings in Palestine at the beginning of the Christian era. But did He really stand before us in all His glory, in His full radiance?' The question arose out of their hearts. 'Was it not only after our death that we learned how Christ had descended from cosmic heights, as a Being of the Sun, to the earth? Did we really experience Him as the Being of the Sun? He is here no longer, He is united with the earth. Here we can only find what is like a great cosmic memory of Him. We must find our way back again to the earth, in order to have the Christ before our souls.'

A longing for Christ accompanied these souls from that time forth, when with the Spirit-Beings of the Hierarchies they wove the mighty and sublime cosmic Imaginations. This longing went with them from their pre-earthly life into the present life on earth.

This can be experienced with overwhelming intensity by spiritual vision when it observes what was taking place in mankind, incarnate and discarnate, in the course of the 19th and 20th centuries. And as I said, all manner of things were mingled into these impressions. For we must remember that in their Christian experience the souls who are now returning had shared in all that was taking place as between those who were striving for Christianity and those who still stood within the old Pagan consciousness,—which was frequently the case during the centuries to which I just now referred. In these souls therefore, many of those influences are present which make it possible for man to fall a victim to the temptations of Lucifer on the one hand and Ahriman on the other. For in karma, Lucifer and Ahriman are weaving, no less than the good gods: this we have already seen.

All that was thus interwoven, and that works itself out karmically to-day, must be followed out in detail, if we would really penetrate the spiritual foundations of anthroposophical striving. If the Christmas Foundation Meeting is to be taken in real earnest, the time has now come when we must draw aside the veil from certain things. Only they must be taken with the necessary earnestness.

Let us begin, as I said, with a radical instance; and while we discuss the following, let there hold sway in the background, for the rest of this hour, all that has now been said.

From the pre-earthly into this earthly existence, through their education, through all that they experience on earth, human souls find their way. They seek and find their way into the Anthroposophical Society, and remain in it for a time. But there are isolated cases among them, where, having shewn themselves zealous, nay over-zealous members of the Anthroposophical Society for a while, they become the most violent opponents. Let us observe the working of karma in an extreme case of this kind.

A person comes into the Anthroposophical Society. He proves a very zealous member, yet after a time he somehow manages to become not only an opponent but a maligner among opponents. We must admit, it is a very strange karma.

We will consider a single case. There is a soul. We look back into a past life on earth, into a time when old memories from the ages of Paganism still lingered on, enticingly for many people. It was a time when men were finding their way on the one hand into a Christianity that spread out with a certain warmth and fire, and yet, for many of them, with a certain superficiality.

When such things are spoken of, we must always remember that we have to begin somewhere or other, at some particular earthly life. Every such earthly life leads back to earlier ones in turn; therefore there will always be some things that remain unexplained—things to which we simply refer as matters of fact. They are of course the karmic consequences of still earlier events, but we have to begin *somewhere.*

In the period to which I have just referred we find a certain soul. We find him, indeed, in a way that very nearly concerned myself and other present members of this Society. We find him as a would-be maker of gold, in possession of writings, manuscripts which he is hardly able to understand but interprets in his own way and then makes experiments in accordance with the instructions, though he has no real notion what he is doing. For it is by no means a simple matter to look into the spiritually chemical relationships, if we may call them so. Thus we see him as an experimenter, with a little library containing the most varied instructions and recipes going far back into Moorish and Arabian sources. We see him unfolding this activity in an almost-out-of-the-way place, though visited by many inquisitive persons. At length, under the influence of the practices in which he engages without understanding, he gets a strange physical debility,—a disease attacking especially the larynx, —and (this being a masculine incarnation) his voice becomes hoarser and hoarser till it has almost vanished.

Meanwhile the Christian teachings are spread abroad; they are taking hold of men on all hands. This man is filled on the one hand with the greedy longing to make gold, and, with the making of gold, to attain many other things attainable at that time if one had been successful in making gold. On the other hand Christianity comes near to him, in a way that is full of reproaches. There arises in him what I may perhaps describe as a kind of Faustian feeling, though not altogether pure. Strong becomes the feeling in him: ' Have I not really done an awful wrong? ' By-and-by under the influence of such reflections the conclusion grows upon him, living with scepticism in his soul: ' Your having lost your voice is the divine punishment, the just punishment, for meddling with unrighteous things.'

In this situation of his inner life, he sought out the advice of human beings who have also become united at this present time with the Anthroposophical Society, and who were able at that time really to play a helpful part in his destiny. For they were able to save his soul from deep and anxious doubt. We can really speak of a certain ' salvation of the soul ' in this case. But all this took place under such conditions that he experienced it with feelings which remained to some extent external, no matter how intense they were. He was overwhelmed on the one hand with a sense of gratitude toward those who had saved his inner life. But on the other hand—unclear as it all was—an appalling Ahrimanic impulse became mingled with it. After the strong inclination towards unrighteous magic practices, and with his present feeling—which was not quite genuine—of having entered into Christian righteousness, an Ahrimanic trait became mixed up in all these things. For in effect the soul was brought into confusion; things were not really clear, and the result was that he brought an Ahrimanic trait into his gratitude. His thankfulness was transformed into something that found an unworthy expression in his soul, and that appeared to him in this light, during his life between death and new birth. It came before him especially when he had reached that point which I described, in the first half of the 19th century. There he had to live through it again; and he experienced the deep unworthiness of what his soul had evolved in that former life, by way of gratitude which was superficial, external, nay even cringing.

We see this picture of Ahrimanised gratitude mixed up in the cosmic Imaginations of which I spoke. And we see the soul descend from that pre-earthly existence into a new earthly life. We see him descend on the one hand with all those impulses that entered into him from the time when he was seeking to make gold,—the materialistic corruption of a spiritual striving. On the other hand we see evolving in him under the Ahrimanic influence something which is distinctly to be perceived as a sense of shame,—shame at his gratitude improperly expressed and superficial.

These two currents live in his soul as he descends to earth. And they express themselves in this way: The soul of whom I am speaking, having become a person again in earthly life, finds his way to those others who were also with him in the first half of the 19th century.

To begin with, a kind of memory arises in him of what he lived through in the Imaginative picture of the unworthy external gratitude. All these things become unfolded now, almost automatically. Then there awakens what is living there within him,—what I described as a sense of shame at his own attitude which had been unworthy of a man. This takes hold of his soul, but, influenced as it is by Ahriman (through the karma of former epochs too, of course), it finds vent as an appalling hatred against all that he had at first espoused. The sense of shame against himself becomes transformed into a wild and angry opposition. And this again is united with dreadful disappointment that all his old subconscious cravings have been so little satisfied. For they would have been satisfied if anything had arisen now, similar to what was contained in the old, improper art of making gold.

You see, my dear friends, here we have a radical example shewing how such things turn inward. We have traced the strange mysterious by-ways of such a thing as this: the connection of a sense of shame with hatred. Such things must also be discovered in the connections of human life if we would understand a present life from its preceding conditions.

When we consider such things as these, a certain measure of understanding is indeed poured out over all that takes place through human beings in the world. Then indeed great difficulties of life begin, when we take the thought of karma in real earnest. But these difficulties are meant to come, for they are founded in the real essence of human life. Such a Movement as the Anthroposophical must indeed be exposed to many things, for only so can it evolve the strong forces which it needs.

I gave you this example first, so that you might see how we must seek—even for negative things—the karmic relationships with the whole stream of destiny which is causing the Anthroposophical Movement to arise out of the preceding incarnations of those who are joined together in this Society.

So, my dear friends, we may hope that there will awaken in us by-and-by an entirely new understanding of the essence of this Anthroposophical Society. We may hope to discover, as it were, the very soul of the Anthroposophical Society with all its many difficulties. For in this case too, we must not remain within the limits of the single human life, but trace it back to what is now being—I cannot say re-incarnated—but re-experienced in life. In this direction I wanted to begin to-day.

IV

The Soul's Condition of those who seek for Anthroposophy

To-day I would like to insert certain things which will afterwards make it possible for us to understand more closely the karmic connections of the Anthroposophical Movement itself. What I wish to say to-day will take its start from the fact that there are two groups of human beings in the Anthroposophical Movement. In general terms I have already described how the Anthroposophical Movement is composed of the individuals within it. What I shall say to-day must of course be taken in broad outline and as a whole; but there *are* the two groups of human beings in the Anthroposophical Movement. The things which I shall characterise do not lie so obviously spread out ' on the palm of the hand,' as we say. They are by no means such that crude and simple observation would enable us to say: in the case of this or that member, it is so or so. Much of what I shall characterise to-day lies not in the full everyday consciousness of the personality, but, like most karmic things, in the instincts—in the sub-consciousness. Nevertheless, it does thoroughly impress itself on the character and temperament, the mode of action and indeed the real action of the human being.

We have to distinguish the one group, who are related to Christianity in such a way that those who belong to it feel their attachment to Christianity nearest and dearest to their hearts. There lives in these souls the longing, as anthroposophists, to be able to call themselves Christians in the true sense of the word, as they conceive it.

This group derives great comfort from the fact that it can be said in the widest and fullest sense: The Anthroposophical Movement is one that recognises and bears the Christ Impulse within it. Indeed, for this group, pangs of conscience would arise if it were not so.

Now as to the other group:—In the manifestations of their life, those who belong to it are indeed no less sincerely Christian. And yet, they come to Christianity from rather a different angle. To begin with they find great satisfaction in the anthroposophical cosmology—the evolution of the earth from the other planetary forms, and so forth. They find satisfaction in all that Anthroposophy has to say about Man in general. From this point they are then led naturally to Christianity. But they do not feel in the same measure an inward need of the heart, to place Christ in the central point at all costs.

As I said, these things work themselves out to a large extent in the subconsciousness. But whoever is able to practice true observation of souls will be able to judge the different individuals in the right way in every single case.

Now the origins of this grouping go back into very ancient times. You know, my dear friends, from my *Occult Science* that at a certain period of earthly evolution the souls took their departure as it were from the continued evolution of the Earth and came to dwell on other planets of our system. Then, during a certain time—during the Lemurian and Atlantean times—they came down again to Earth. Thus the souls came down again from the various planets—not only from Jupiter, Saturn, Mars, etc., but also from the Sun —to take on an earthly form. And we know how there arose, under the influence of these facts, what I described in *Occult Science* as the Oracles.

Now there were many among these souls who tended through a very ancient karma to come into that stream which afterwards became the Christian stream. We must remember, after all, that less than a third of the population of the earth are professing Christians to this day. Thus only a certain number of the individual souls who came down to earth unfolded the tendency, the impulse, to evolve towards the Christian stream.

The human souls came down at different times. There were those who came down comparatively soon, in the first periods of Atlantean civilisation. But there were also those who came down relatively late—whose sojourn, so to speak, in the pre-earthly, planetary life was long. When we look back into the life of such a soul—beginning with the present incarnation—we come perhaps to a former Christian incarnation and maybe to yet another Christian incarnation. Then we come to the pre-Christian incarnations. But we reach comparatively soon the earliest incarnation of such a soul, whereat we must say: Tracing the life still farther back from this point, it goes up into the planetary realms. Before this point, these souls were not yet present in earthly incarnations.

In the case of other souls, who have also found their way into Christianity, it is different. We can go very far back; we find many incarnations. It was after many incarnations, pre-Christian and Atlantean too, that these other souls dived down at length into the Christian stream.

For intellectualistic thought, such a thing as I have just mentioned is exceedingly misleading. For one might easily be led to suppose that those who by the judgment of present-day civilisation would be considered as particularly able minds, are the very ones who have had many incarnations. But this need not by any means be the case. On the contrary, people who have excellent faculties in the present-day sense of the word—people who are well able to enter into modern life, may often be the very ones for whom we find comparatively few past incarnations on the earth.

Perhaps I may here remind you of what I said at the time when the anthroposophical stream which we now have in the Anthroposophical Movement was inaugurated. I may remind you of what I said at the Christmas Foundation Meeting, when I spoke of those individualities with whom the Epic of Gilgamesh is connected.* I explained certain things about such individualities. We find, as we look

* See *World History in the Light of Anthroposophy.* Rudolf Steiner Press, 1977.

backward, that they had had comparatively few incarnations.

Now, my dear friends, for those human souls who come to Anthroposophy to-day—no matter whether there are still other, intermediate incarnations or not—that incarnation is important, which falls roughly into the 3rd or 4th or 5th century after Christ. (We find it nearly always, spread out over a fairly long period,—two to three centuries. Sometimes it is later—even as late as the 7th or 8th century). Above all things, we must look into the experiences of these souls in that early Christian time. We then find a subsequent incarnation when all these experiences were fastened or confirmed. But I will connect what now I have to say to-day most definitely with what we may describe as the first Christian incarnation.

Now in the case of all these souls, the important thing is: According to all their past conditions, their former lives on earth, how were they to relate themselves to Christianity? You see, my dear friends, this is a very important karmic question. Later on we shall have to consider other, more subsidiary karmic questions; but this question is so to speak a cardinal question of karma, because, passing over many other subsidiary things, it is through their deepest, innermost experiences in former incarnations—through what they underwent with respect to world-conceptions, religious beliefs and the like—that human beings come into the Anthroposophical Society. With respect to the karma of the Anthroposophical Society, this must therefore be placed into the foreground. What have the souls in this Society experienced, in matters of Knowledge, World-conception and Religion?

Now in those early centuries of Christian evolution, one could still take one's start from traditions of knowledge—which had existed ever since the founding of Christianity—about the Being of Christ Himself. In these traditions, He who lived as Christ in the personality of Jesus was regarded as a Dweller on the Sun, a Being of the Sun, before He entered into this earthly life. We must not imagine that the attitude of the Christian world to these truths was always as negative as it is to-day. In the first centuries of Christianity they still understood the Gospels, certain passages of which speak so distinctly of this Mystery. They understood that the Being who is called Christ had come down into a human body from the Sun. How they conceived it in detail is less important for the moment; the point is that this conception was still theirs. It certainly went as far as I have just described.

At the same time, in the epoch of which I am now speaking, the possibility of really understanding such a conception had dwindled very much. It was hard to understand that a Being coming from the Sun descends on to the Earth. Above all, many of the souls who had come into Christianity having a large number of earthly incarnations behind them—far back into Atlantean times—could no longer fully understand how Christ can be called a Being of the Sun. The very souls who in their old beliefs had felt themselves attached to the Sun-Oracles, and who thus revered the Christ even in Atlantean times inasmuch as they looked upward to the Sun—the souls therefore who according to the saying of St. Augustine were 'Christians before Christianity was founded upon Earth,'* Christians as it were of the Sun—these very souls, by the whole character of their spiritual life, could find no real understanding of the saying that Christ was a Sun-Hero. Therefore they preferred to hold fast to that belief which—without such interpretation,

* St. Augustine: *Retractationes.* I.xiii.3.

"When I said [in his book *De Vera Religione*] 'That is in our times the Christian religion, to know which, is the most secure and certain salvation,' it was said in relation to the name, not in relation to the thing itself, of which it is the name. For the thing itself, which is now called the Christian religion, was there among the people of antiquity, and was not wanting from the beginning of the human race, down to the time when Christ came in the flesh; whereafter the true religion, which was always there, began to be called Christian. For when the Apostles began to preach Him after the resurrection and ascension into heaven, and very many believed, first of all at Antioch, as it is written, they were called Christian disciples (Acts XI, 26). Therefore I said: 'This is in our times the Christian religion,' not because it was not there in earlier times, but because in later times it received this name." (Tr. from the Latin text).

without this cosmic Christology—simply regarded Christ as a God, a God from unknown realms, who had united Himself with the body of Jesus. Under these conditions, they accepted what is related in the Gospels. They could no longer turn their gaze upward to the cosmic worlds in order to understand the Being of the Christ. They had learned to know Him only in the worlds beyond the Earth. For even the Mysteries on Earth—the Sun-Oracles—had always spoken to them of Christ as a Sun-Being. Thus they could not find their way into the idea that Christ—this Christ beyond the Earth—had really become an earthly Being.

These Christian souls, when they afterwards passed through the gate of death, came into a strange position, which I may describe—somewhat tritely perhaps—as follows. These Christians, in their life after death, came into the position of a man who knows the name of another man and has heard many things about him; but he has never made his acquaintance in person. To such a man it may happen, at a moment when all the support which served him as long as he merely knew of the *name* are taken away, that he is suddenly expected to know the real person, and his inner life completely fails him in face of this new situation. So it was with the souls of whom I have now spoken: those who in ancient times had felt themselves belonging especially to the Sun-Oracles. In their life after death, they came into a situation in which they had to say, 'Where, then, *is* the Christ? We are now among the Beings of the Sun, where we had always found Him, but now we find Him not.' That He was on Earth, this they had not really received into the thoughts and feelings which remained to them when they passed through the gate of death. So after death they found themselves in a state of great uncertainty about the Christ and they lived on in this uncertainty about Him. They remained in many respects in this uncertainty. Thus, if in the intervening time another incarnation followed, they tended easily to join those groups of men who are described to us in the religious history of Europe as the various heretical societies.

Then, no matter whether they had passed through such another incarnation or not, they found themselves together again in that great gathering above the earth, which I described here the other morning, placing it at the time of the first half of the 19th century. Then it was that these souls among others found themselves face to face with a great supersensible cult or ritual, consisting in mighty Imaginations. And in the sublime Imaginations of that supersensible ritual there was enacted before their spiritual vision, above all other things, the great Sun-Mystery of Christ. These souls, as I explained, had as it were come to a blind alley with their Christianity. And the object was, before they should descend to earthly life again, to bring them, in picture-form at least, face to face with Christ, whom they had lost—though not entirely—yet to such extent that in their souls He had become involved in currents of uncertainty and doubt.

Now these souls responded in a peculiar way. Not that they found themselves in a still greater uncertainty through the fact that all this was enacted before them. On the contrary it gave them a certain satisfaction in their life between death and a new birth—a feeling of salvation from many doubts. But it also gave them a kind of memory of what they had received about the Christ—albeit in a form that had not yet been permeated in the true cosmic sense by the Mystery of Golgotha. Thus there remained in their inmost being an immense warmth and devotion of feeling towards Christianity, and at the same time a subconscious dawning of those sublime Imaginations.

All this was concentrated into a great longing, that they might now at last be able to be Christians in the true way. Then when they descended—when they became young again, returning to the earth at the end of the 19th or at the turn of the 19th and 20th centuries—having received the Christ by way of inner feeling though without cosmic understanding in their early Christian incarnation, they could do no other than feel themselves impelled towards Him. But the impressions they had received in the Imaginations to which they had been drawn in their pre-earthly life, remained in them only as an undefined longing. Thus it was difficult for them to find their way into the anthroposophical world-conception, inasmuch as the latter studies the cosmos to begin with and leaves the consideration of Christ until a later point.

Why did they have such difficulty? For the simple reason, my dear friends, that they had their own peculiar relationship to the question 'What is Anthroposophy?' Let us ask: What is Anthroposophy in its reality? My dear friends, if you gaze into all those wonderful, majestic Imaginations that stood there as a supersensible spiritual action in the first half of the 19th century, and if you translate all these into human concepts, then you have Anthroposophy. For the next higher level of experience—for the adjoining spiritual world whence man descends into this earthly life—Anthroposophy was already there in the first half of the 19th century. It was not on the earth, but it was there. And if Anthroposophy is seen to-day it is seen indeed in that direction: towards the first half of the 19th century. Quite as a matter of course one sees it there. Nay, even at the end of the 18th century one sees it.

For example, one may have the following experience. There was a certain man who was once in a peculiar position. Through a friend, the great riddle of human earthly life was raised before him. But this his friend was not altogether free of the angular thinking of Kant ("das kantige Kant'sche Denken"), and thus it came to expression in a rather abstract philosophic way. He himself—the one of whom I am now speaking—could not find his way into the 'angular thinking of Kant.' Yet everything in his soul stirred up the same great riddle, the great question of life. How are the reason and the sensuous nature of man connected with one another? And lo, there were opened to him—not merely the doors but the very flood-gates, which for a moment let radiate into his soul those regions of the World in which the mighty Imaginations were being enacted. And all this—entering not through windows or doors but through wide-open flood-gates into his soul—translated as it were into little miniatures, came forth as the fairy-tale of the Green Snake and the Beautiful Lily. For the man of whom I speak was Goethe.

Miniatures—tiny reflected images, translated even into a fairy-like prettiness—descended thus in Goethe's Tale of the Green Snake and the Beautiful Lily. We need not therefore wonder that when it became necessary to give Anthroposophy in artistic scenes or pictures, (where we too must naturally have recourse to the great Imaginations), my first Mystery Play, 'The Portal of Initiation' became alike in structure—albeit different in content—alike in structure to the Fairy Tale of the Green Snake and the Beautiful Lily.

You see it is possible to look into the deeper connection even through the actual things that have taken place among us. Everyone who has had anything to do with occult matters, knows that that which happens on earth is the downward reflection of something that has taken place long, long before in the spiritual world, though in a somewhat different way, inasmuch as certain spirits of hindrance are not mingled in it there.

These souls now, who were preparing to descend into earthly existence at the end of the 19th or at the beginning of the 20th century, brought with them—albeit in their subconsciousness—a longing also to know something of cosmology, etc., *i.e.* to look out upon the world in the anthroposophical way. But above all things, their heart and mind were strongly inflamed for Christ. They would have felt pangs of conscience if this whole conception of Anthroposophy—to which they found themselves attracted as an outcome of their pre-earthly life—had not been permeated by the Christ Impulse. Such was the one group, taken of course 'as a whole.'

The other group lived differently. If I may put it so, the other group, when they emerged in their present incarnation, had not yet reached that weariness in Paganism which the souls whom I described just now had reached. Compared to those others, they had indeed spent a relatively short time on earth—they had had fewer incarnations; and in these incarnations they had filled themselves with the mighty impulses which a man may have, if through his lives on earth he has stood in a living connection with the many Pagan Gods, and if this connnection echoes strongly in his later incarnations. Thus they were not yet weary of the old Paganism. Even in the first centuries of Christianity the old Pagan impulses had still been working in them strongly, although they did incline more or less to Christianity, which, as we know, only gradually worked its way forth from Paganism.

At that time they received Christianity chiefly through their intellect. Though indeed it was intellect permeated with inner feeling, still they received it with their intellect. They thought a great deal about Christianity. Nor must you imagine this a very learned kind of thinking. They may indeed have been relatively simple men and women, in simple circumstances; but they thought much.

Once again it matters not whether there was a subsequent incarnation in the meantime. Such an incarnation will of course have wrought some changes; but the essential thing is this: When they had passed through the gate of death, these souls looked back upon the earth in such a way that Christianity appeared to them as something into which they had not yet really grown. They were less weary of the old Paganism; they still bore within their souls strong impulses from the old Pagan life. Thus they were still waiting, as it were, for the time when they should become true Christians.

The very people of whom I spoke to you a week ago, describing how they battled against Paganism on the side of Christianity—they themselves were among the souls who in reality still bore much Paganism, many Pagan impulses within them. They were still waiting to become real Christians. These souls, then, passed through the gate of death. They arrived in the spiritual world. They passed through the life between death and a new birth, and in the time which I have indicated—in the first half of the 19th century or a little earlier—they came before that sublime and glorious Imagination; and in these Imaginations they beheld so many impulses to fire their work and their activity. They received these impulses paramountly into their will.

And, if I may say so, when we now look with occult vision at all that these souls are carrying to-day, especially within their will, we find—above all in their life of will—the frequent impress of those mighty spiritual Imaginations.

Now the souls who enter their earthly life in such condition feel the need, to begin with, to experience again here upon earth—in the way that is possible on earth—what they experienced in their pre-earthly life as a determining factor for their karmic work. For the former kind, for the former group of souls, the life in the first half of the 19th century took its course in such a way that they felt themselves impelled by a deep longing to partake in that supersensible cult or ritual. Yet they came to it—if I may so describe it—in a vague and mystic mood, so that when they afterwards descended to the earth, only dim recollections remained to them; albeit Anthroposophy, transformed into its earthly shape, could make itself intelligible to them through these recollections. But with the second group it was different. It was as though they found themselves together again in the living after-effect of the resolve that they had made. For they, even then, had not been quite weary of Paganism. They still stood in expectation of being able to become Christians in a true way of evolution. And now it was as though they remembered a resolve that they had made during that first half of the 19th century: a resolve to carry down on to the earth all that had stood before them in such mighty pictures, and to translate it into an earthly form.

When we look at many an anthroposophist who bears within him the impulse above all to work and co-operate with Anthroposophy most actively, we find among such anthroposophists souls of the kind that I have now described. The two types can be distinguished very clearly.

Now, my dear friends, perhaps you will say: All that you have here told us may explain many things in the karma of the Anthroposophical Society; but one may well grow anxious: 'What is coming next?'—seeing that so many things are being explained about which one might well prefer not to be torn away from blissful ignorance. Are we now to set to work and think, whether we belong to the one type or the other? My dear friends, to this I must give a very definite answer. If the Anthroposophical Society were merely to contain a theoretic teaching or a confession of belief in such and such ideas of cosmology, Christology, etc.—if such were the character of this Society—it would certainly not be what it is intended to be by those who stand at its fountain-head. Anthroposophy shall be something which for a true anthroposophist has power to change and transform his life, to carry into the Spiritual what is experienced nowadays only in unspiritual forms of expression.

I will ask you this: Has it a very bad effect upon a child when at a certain age certain things are explained to him or her? Until a certain age is reached, the children do not know whether they are French or Germans, Norwegians,—Belgians or Italians. At any rate this whole way of thinking has little meaning for them until a certain age. One may say, they know nothing of it in reality. We need only put it radically:—You will surely not have met many Chauvinist babies, or even three-year old Chauvinists! . . . It is only at a certain age that we become aware: I am German, I am a Frenchman, I am an Englishman, I am a Dutchman and so on. Yet in accepting these things, do we not grow into them quite naturally? Do we say it is a thing unbearable, to discover at a certain age of childhood that we are a Pole or a Frenchman, or a German or a Russian or a Dutchman? . . . . . We are used to these things, we take them as a matter of course. But this, my dear friends, is in the external realm of the senses. Anthroposophy is to raise the whole life of man to a higher level. We must learn to bear different things, things which will only shock us in the life of the senses if we misunderstand them. And among the things we are to learn to recognise there is this too:—We must grow just as naturally and simply into the self-knowledge which is to realise that we belong to the one type or the other.

By this means too, the foundation will be created for a right estimation of the other karmic impulses in our lives. Hence it was necessary, as a kind of first direction, to show how the individual—according to the special manner of his pre-destination—stands in relation to this Anthroposophy, to this Christology, and in relation to the greater degree of activity or passivity within the Anthroposophical Movement.

Of course there are transitions too, between the one type and the other. These however are due to the fact that that which comes over from the previous incarnation into the present is still irradiated by a yet earlier incarnation. Especially with the souls of the second group, this is often the case. Many things still shine over from their genuinely heathen incarnations. For this reason they have a very definite pre-disposition to take the Christ in the sense in which He must truly be taken, namely as a Cosmic Being. But what I am now saying shows itself not so very much in the ideal considerations; it shows itself far more in the practical things of life. The two types can be recognised far better by the way in which they tackle the detailed situations of life than by their thoughts. Thoughts indeed have no great significance—I mean, the abstract thoughts have no such great significance for man. So, for instance (needless to say, the personal element is always to be excluded here) we shall frequently find the transition types from the one to the other among those who somehow cannot help carrying over the habits of non-anthroposophical life into the Anthroposophical Movement. I mean, those who are not even inclined to take the Anthroposophical Movement so very seriously, and those above all who are always grumbling in the Anthroposophical Movement, finding fault with the anthroposophists. Precisely among those who are always finding fault with the conditions in the Anthroposophical Movement, especially with the personalities and all the little petty things, we find the transition types, flickering from the one into the other. For in such cases the intensity of neither of the two impulses is very strong.

Therefore, my dear friends, at all costs—even though it may sometimes mean a searching of conscience and character—we must somehow find it possible, each one of us, to deepen the Anthroposophical Movement in this direction, approaching such realities as these and thinking a little earnestly on this: How do we, according to our own supersensible nature, belong to the Anthroposophical Movement? If we do this, there will arise a purer conception of the Anthroposophical Movement; it will become in course of time an ever more spiritual conception. What we have hitherto maintained in theory—and it need not go so very deep, when we merely stand for it as a theory—this we shall now apply to real life. It is indeed an intense application to life, when we learn to place ourselves, our own life, into connection with these things. To talk a lot of karma, saying that such and such things are punished or rewarded thus and thus from one life to the next, need not strike so very deep; it need not hurt us. But when it reaches so to speak into our own flesh and blood—when it is a question of placing our own present incarnation, with the perfectly definite supersensible quality that underlies it—then indeed it goes far nearer to our being. And it is this deepening of the human being which we must bring into all earthly life, into all earthly civilisation through Anthroposophy.

This, my dear friends, was a kind of Intermezzo in our studies, and we will continue from this point next Friday.

V

SPIRITUAL CONDITIONS OF EVOLUTION LEADING UP TO THE ANTHROPOSOPHICAL MOVEMENT

The members of the Anthroposophical Society come into the Society, as indeed is obvious, for reasons that lie in their inner life, in the inner condition of their souls. And as we are now speaking of the karma of the Anthroposophical Society, nay of the Anthroposophical Movement altogether, showing how it arises out of the karmic evolution of members and groups of members, we shall need to perceive the foundations of this karma above all in the state of soul of those human beings who seek for Anthroposophy. This we have already begun to do, and we will now acquaint ourselves with certain other facts in this direction, so that we may enter still further into the karma of the Anthroposophical Movement.

Most important in the soul-condition of anthroposophists, as I have already said, are the experiences which they underwent in their incarnations during the first centuries of the founding of Christianity. As I said, there may have been other intervening incarnations; but that incarnation is above all important, which we find, approximately, in the fourth, fifth, sixth, seventh, or eighth century A.D. In considering this incarnation we found that we must distinguish two groups among the human beings who come to the Anthroposophical Movement. These two groups we have already characterised. We are now going to consider something which they have in common. We shall consider a significant common element, lying at the foundation of the souls who have undergone such lines of evolution as I described in the last lecture.

Looking at the first Christian centuries, we find ourselves

in an age when men were very different from what they are to-day. When the man of to-day awakens from sleep, he slips down into his physical body with great rapidity, though with the reservation which I mentioned here not long ago, when I said that this entry and expansion into the physical body really lasts the whole day long. Be that as it may, the *perception* that the Ego and the astral body are approaching takes place very quickly. For the awakening human being in the present age, there is, so to speak, no intervening time between the becoming-aware of the etheric body and the becoming-aware of the physical. Man passes rapidly through the perception of the etheric body—simply does not notice the etheric body,—and dives down at once into the physical. This is a peculiarity of the man of the present time.

The nature of the human beings who lived in those early Christian centuries was different. When they awoke from sleep they had a distinct perception: " I am entering a twofold entity: the etheric body and the physical." They knew that man first passes through the perception of the etheric body, and then only enters into the physical. Thus indeed, in their moment of awakening they had before them—though not a complete tableau of life—still very many pictures of their past earthly life. And they had before them another thing, which I shall describe directly. For if man enters thus, stage by stage, into that which remains lying on the couch, into the etheric and physical bodies,—the result is that the whole period of waking life becomes very different from the experiences which we have in our waking life to-day.

Again, when we consider the moment of falling asleep nowadays, the peculiar thing is this:—when the Ego and astral body leave the physical and etheric, the Ego very quickly absorbs the astral body. And as the Ego confronts the cosmos without any kind of support, being unable at its present stage to perceive anything at all, man as he falls asleep ceases to have perceptions. For the little that emerges in his dreams is quite sporadic.

This again was not so in the times of which I am now speaking. The Ego did not at once absorb the astral body; the astral body continued to exist, independently in its own substance, even after the human being had fallen asleep. And to a certain extent, it remained so through the whole night. Thus in the morning the human being awakened not from utter darkness of unconsciousness, but with the feeling:—"I have been living in a world filled with light, in which all manner of things were happening." Albeit they were only pictures, something was taking place there. It was so indeed: the man of that time had an intermediate feeling, an intermediate sensation between sleeping and waking. It was delicate, it was light and intimate, but it was there. It was only with the beginning of the 14th century that this condition ceased completely in civilised mankind.

Now this means that all the souls, of whose life I was speaking the other day, experienced the world differently from the man of the present time. Let us try to understand, my dear friends, how those human beings—that is to say you yourselves, all of you, during that time—experienced the world.

The diving down into the etheric and physical body took place in distinct stages. And the effect of this was that throughout his waking life man looked out upon Nature differently. He saw not the bare, prosaic, matter-of-fact world of the senses, seen by the man of modern times, who—if he would make any more of it—can only do so by his fancy or imagination. No, when the man of that time looked out, upon the world of plants, for instance, he saw the flowering meadow land as though there were spread over it a slight and gentle bluish-red cloud-halo. Especially at the time of day when the sun was shining less brightly (not at the height of noon-tide), it was as though a bluish-red light, like a luminous mist with manifold and moving waves and colours, were spread over the flowering meadow. What we see to-day, when a slight mist hangs over the meadow (which comes of course from evaporated water), —such a thing was seen at that time in the spiritual, in the astral. Indeed every tree-top was seen enveloped in a cloud, and when man saw the fields of corn, it was as though bluey-red rays were descending from the cosmos, springing forth in clouds of mist, descending into the soil of the earth.

And when man looked at the animals, he had not merely an impression of the physical shape, but the physical was enveloped in an astral aura. Slightly, delicately, and only intimately, this aura was seen. Nay, it was only seen when the sunshine light was working in a rather gentle way;—but seen it was. Thus everywhere in outer Nature man still perceived the spiritual, working and weaving.

Then, when he died, the experience he had in the first days after passing through the gate of death—gazing back upon the whole of his past earthly life—was in reality not unfamiliar to him. As he looked back upon his earthly life directly after death, he had a distinct feeling. He said to himself: Now I am letting go that quality, that aura from my own organism, which goes out into all that I have seen of the aura in external Nature. My etheric body goes to its own home. Such was man's feeling.

Naturally all these feelings had been much stronger in more ancient times. But they still existed—though in a slight and delicate form—in the time of which I am now speaking. And when man beheld these things directly after passing through the gate of death, he had the feeling: " In all the spiritual life and movement which I have seen hovering over the things and processes of Nature, the Word of the Father-God is speaking. My etheric body is going to the Father."

And if man thus saw the outer world of Nature differently owing to the different mode of his awakening, so too he saw his own outer form differently than in subsequent ages. When he fell asleep the astral body was not immediately absorbed by the Ego. Now under such conditions the astral body itself is filled with sound. Thus from spiritual worlds there sounded into the sleeping human Ego,—though no longer so distinctly as in ancient times, still in a gentle and intimate way,—all manner of things which cannot be heard in the waking state. And on awakening man had the very real feeling: It was a language of spiritual Beings in the light-filled spaces of the cosmos in which I partook between my falling asleep and my awakening.

And when man had laid aside the etheric body a few days after passing through the gate of death, to live henceforth in his astral body, he had once more this feeling: " In my astral body I now experience in a returning course all that I thought and did on earth. In this astral body in which I lived every night during my sleep,—herein I am experiencing all that I thought and did on earth." Moreover, while he had carried into his awakening moments only a vague and undetermined feeling, he now had a far clearer feeling. Now in the time between death and a new birth, as in his astral body he returned through his past earthly life, he had the feeling: " Behold in this my astral body lives the Christ. I only did not notice it, but in reality every night my astral body dwelt in the essence and being of the Christ." Now man knew, that for as long as he would have to go thus backward through his earthly life Christ would not desert him, for Christ was with his astral body.

My dear friends, it is so indeed, whatever may have been one's attitude to Christianity in those first Christian centuries, whether it was like the first group of whom I spoke or like the second, whether one had still lived as it were with the more Pagan strength, or with the weariness of Paganism, one was sure to experience—if not on earth, then after death —the great fact of the Mystery of Golgotha; Christ who had been the ruling Being of the Sun, had united Himself with what lives as humanity on earth. Such was the experience of all who had come in any way near to Christianity in the first centuries of Christian evolution. For the others, these experiences after their death remained more or less unintelligible.

Such were the fundamental differences in the experience of souls in the first Christian centuries, and afterwards. Now all this had another effect as well. For when man looked out upon the world of Nature in his waking life, he felt this world of Nature as the essential domain of the Father God. All the spiritual that he beheld living and moving there, was for him the expression, the manifestation and the glory of the Father God. And he felt: This world, in the time when Christ appeared on earth, stood verily in need of something. It was the need that Christ should be received into the substance of the earth for mankind. In relation to all the processes of Nature and the whole realm of Nature, man still had the feeling of a living principle of Christ. For indeed, his perception of Nature, inasmuch as he beheld a spiritual living and moving and holding sway there, involved something else as well. All this which he felt as a spiritual living and moving and holding sway,—hovering in ever-changing spirit-shapes over all plant and animal existence,—all this he felt so that with simple and unbiassed human feeling he would describe it in the words: It is the innocence of Nature's being. Yes, my dear friends, what he could thus spiritually see was called in truth: the innocence in the kingdom of Nature. He spoke of the pure and innocent spirituality in all the working of Nature.

But the other thing, which he felt inwardly—feeling when he awakened that in his sleep he had been in a world of light and sounding spiritual being—of this he felt that good, and evil too, might there prevail. In this he felt, as it sounded forth from the depths of spiritual being, good spirits and evil spirits too were speaking. Of the good spirits he felt that they only wanted to raise to a higher level the innocence of Nature and to preserve it; but the evil spirits wanted to adulterate with guilt this guiltlessness of Nature. Wherever such Christians lived as I am now describing, the powers of good and evil were felt through the very fact that as man slept the Ego was not drawn in and absorbed into the astral body.

Not all who called themselves Christians in that time, or who were in any way near to Christianity, were in this state of soul. Nevertheless there were many people living in the southern and middle regions of Europe, who said: " Verily, my inner being that lives its independent life from the time

I fall asleep till I awaken, belongs to the region of a good and to the region of an evil world." Again and again men thought and pondered about the depth of the forces that bring forth the good and the evil in the human soul. Heavily they felt the fact that the human soul is placed into a world where good and evil powers battle with one another. In the very first centuries of Christianity, such feelings were not yet present in the southern and middle regions of Europe, but in the fifth and sixth centuries they became more and more frequent. Especially among those who received knowledge and teachings from the East (and as we know such teachings from the East came over in manifold ways), this mood of soul arose. It was especially widespread in those regions to which the name Bulgaria afterwards came to be applied. (In a strange way the name persisted even though quite different peoples inhabited these regions). Thus in later centuries, and indeed for a very long time in Europe, those in whom this mood of soul was most strongly developed were called ' Bulgars.' ' Bulgars '—for the people of Western and Middle Europe in the later Christian centuries of the first half of the Middle Ages—Bulgars were human beings who were most strongly touched by this opposition of the good and evil cosmic spiritual powers.

Throughout Europe we find the name ' Bulgar ' applied to human beings such as I have characterised. Now the souls of whom I am here speaking, had been to a greater or lesser degree in this very mood of soul. I mean the souls who in the further course of their development beheld those mighty pictures in the supersensible ceremony, in which they themselves actively took part,—all of which happened in the spiritual world in the first half of the 19th century. All that they had lived through when they had known themselves immersed in the battle between good and evil, was carried by them through their life between death and a new birth. And this gave a certain shade and colouring to these souls as they stood before the mighty cosmic pictures.

To all this yet another thing was added. These souls were indeed the last in European civilisation to preserve a little of that distinct perception of the etheric and the astral body in waking and sleeping. Recognising one another by these common peculiarities of their inner life, they had generally lived in communities. And among the other Christians, who became more and more attached to Rome, they were regarded as heretics. Heretics were not yet condemned as harshly as in later centuries. Still, they were regarded as heretics. Indeed the others always had a certain uncanny feeling about them. They had the impression that these people saw more than other folk. It was as though they were related to the Divine in a different way through the fact that they perceived the sleeping state differently than the others among whom they dwelt. For the others had long lost this faculty and had approached more nearly to the condition of soul which became general in Europe in the 14th century.

Now when these human beings—who had the distinct perception of the astral and the etheric body—passed through the gate of death, then also they were different from the others. Nor must we imagine, my dear friends, that man between death and a new birth is altogether without share in what is taking place through human beings on the earth. Just as we look up from here into the spiritual world of heaven, so between death and a new birth man looks down from that world on to the earth. Just as we here partake with interest in the life of spiritual beings, so from the spiritual world one partakes in the experiences of earthly beings upon the earth. After the age which I have hitherto been describing there came the time when Christendom in Europe was arranging its existence under the assumption that man has no longer any knowledge of his astral or his etheric body. Christianity was now preparing to speak about the spiritual worlds without being able to presume any such knowledge or consciousness among men. For you must think, my dear friends, when the early Christian teachers, in the first few centuries, spoke to *their* Christians—though they already found a large number who were only able to accept the truth of their words by external authority—nevertheless the simpler, more child-like feeling of that time enabled men to accept such words, when spoken from a warm and enthusiastic heart. And of the warmth and enthusiasm of heart with which the men of those first Christian centuries could preach, people to-day, where so much has gone into the mere preaching-of-words, have no conception. Those however who were still able to speak to souls such as I have described to-day,—what kind of words could *they* speak? They, my dear friends, could say: " Behold what shows itself in the rainbow-shining glory over the plants, what shows itself as the desire-nature about the animals,—lo, this is the reflection, this is the manifestation of the spiritual world from which the Christ has come." Speaking to such men about the truths of spiritual wisdom, they could speak, not as of a thing unknown, but in such a way as to remind their hearers of what they could still behold under certain conditions in the gently luminous light of the sun: The Spirit in the world of Nature. Again when they spoke to them of the Gospels which tell of spiritual worlds and spiritual Mysteries or of the secrets of the Old Testament, then again they spoke to them not as of a thing unknown, but they could say: " Here is the Word of the Testament. It has been written down by human beings, who heard, more fully and clearly than you, the whispered language of that spiritual world in which your souls are dwelling from the time you fall asleep till you awaken. But you too know something of this language, for you remember it when you awaken in the morning." Thus it was possible to speak to them of the spiritual as of something known to them. In the conversation of the priests or preachers of that time with these men, something was contained of what was already going on in their own souls. So in that time the Word was still alive and could be cultivated in a living way.

Then when these souls, to whom one had still been able to speak in the *living* Word, had passed through the gate of death, they looked down again upon the earth, and beheld the evening twilight of the living Word below. And they had the feeling that it was the twilight of the Logos. " The

Logos is darkening "—such was the underlying feeling in their souls. After their life in the 7th, 8th or 9th century (or somewhat earlier) when they had passed through the gate of death again and looked down upon the earth, they felt: " Down there upon the earth is the evening twilight of the living Logos." Well may there have lived in these souls the Word: "And the Word became flesh and dwelt among us. But human beings are less and less able to afford a home, a dwelling place for the Word that is to live within the flesh, that is to live on upon the earth." This, I say again, was an underlying mood, it was indeed *the* dominant feeling among these souls, as they lived in the spiritual world between the 7th or 8th and the 19th or 20th century, no matter whether their sojourn there was interrupted by another life on earth. It remained their fundamental underlying feeling: " Christ lives indeed for the earth, since for the earth He died; but the earth cannot receive Him. Somehow there must arise on earth the power for souls to be able to receive the Christ."

Beside all the other things I have described, this feeling became more and more living in the souls who had been stigmatised during their earthly time as heretics. This feeling grew in them between their death and the coming of a renewed revelation of the Christ—a new declaration of His Being.

In this condition of their souls, these human beings—disembodied as they were—witnessed what was happening on earth. It was something hitherto unknown to them, nevertheless they learned to understand what was going on on earth below. They saw how souls on earth were less and less taken hold of by the spirit, till there were no more human beings left, to whom it was possible to speak such words as these: ' We tell you of the Spirit whom you yourselves can still behold hovering over the world of plants, gleaming around the animals. We instruct you in the Testament that was written out of the spiritual sounds whose whispering you still can hear when you feel the echo of your experiences of the night.' This was no more.

Looking down from above they saw how different these

things were now becoming. For in the development of Christendom a substitute was being introduced for the old way of speaking. For a long time, though the vast majority to whom the preachers spoke had no longer any direct consciousness of the Spiritual in their earthly life, still the whole tradition, the whole custom of their speech came down to them from the older times,—I mean, from the time when one knew, as one spoke to men about the Spirit, that they themselves still had some feeling of what it was. It was only about the 9th, 10th or 11th century that these things vanished altogether. Then there arose quite a different condition, even in the listener. Until that time, when a man listened to another, who, filled with a divine enthusiasm, spoke out of the Spirit, he had the feeling as he listened that he was going a little out of himself. He was going out a little, into his etheric body. He was leaving the physical body to a slight extent. He was approaching the astral body more nearly. It was literally true, men still had a slight feeling of being 'transported' as they listened. Nor did they care so very much in those times for the mere hearing of words. What they valued most was the inward experience, however slight, of being transported—carried away. Men experienced with living sympathy the words that were spoken by a God-inspired man.

But from the 9th, 10th, or 11th, and towards the 14th century, this vanished altogether. The mere listening became more and more common. Therefore the need arose to make one's appeal to something different, when one spoke of spiritual things. The need arose somehow to draw forth from the listener what one wanted him to have as a conception of the spiritual world. The need arose as it were to work upon him, until at length he should feel impelled even out of his hardened body to say something about the spiritual world. Thus there arose the need to give instruction about spiritual things in the play of question and answer. There is always a suggestive element in questions. And when one asked: What is baptism? Having prepared the human being so that he would give a certain answer; or when one asked: What is Confirmation? What is the Holy Spirit? What are the seven deadly sins?—when one trained them in this play of question and answer, one provided a substitute for the simple elemental listening. To begin with this was done with those who entered the Schools where this was first made possible. Through question and answer, what they had to say about the spiritual worlds was thoroughly brought home to them. In this way the Catechism arose.

We must indeed look at such events as this. For these things were really witnessed by the souls who were up there in the spiritual world and who now looked down to the earth. They said to themselves: something must now approach man which it was quite impossible for us to know in our lives, for it did not lie near to us at all.

It was a mighty impression when the Catechism was arising down upon the earth. Very little is given when historians outwardly describe the rise of the Catechism, but much is given, my dear friends, when we behold it as it appeared from the supersensible: " Down there upon the earth men are having to undergo things altogether new in the very depths of their souls; they are having to learn by way of Catechism what they are to believe." Herewith I have described a certain feeling, but there is another which I must describe to you as follows:—We must go back once more into the first centuries of Christendom. In those times it was not yet possible for a Christian simply to go into a church, to sit down or to kneel, and then to hear the Mass right through from the beginning—from the " Introitus " —to the prayers which follow the Holy Communion. It was not possible for all Christians to attend the whole Mass through. Those who became Christians were divided into two groups. There were the Catechumenoi who were allowed to attend the Mass till the reading of the Gospel was over. After the Gospel the Offertory was prepared, and then they had to leave. Only those who had been prepared for a considerable time for the holy inner feeling in which one was allowed to behold the Mystery of Transubstantiation, only these—the Transubstantii as they were called—were allowed to remain and hear the Mass through to the end.

That was a very different way of partaking in the Mass. Now the human beings of whom we have been speaking (who in their souls underwent the conditions I described, who looked down on to the earth and perceived this strange Catechism-teaching, which would have been so impossible for them)—they, in their religious worship too, had more or less preserved the old Christian custom of not allowing a man to take part in the whole Mass till he had undergone a longer preparation. They were still conscious of an exoteric and an esoteric portion in the Mass. They regarded as esoteric all that was done from the Transubstantiation onward.

Now once more they looked down and beheld what was going on in the outer ritual of Christendom. They saw that the whole Mass had become exoteric. The whole Mass was being enacted even before those who had not entered into any special mood of soul by special preparation. " Can a man on earth really approach the Mystery of Golgotha, if in unconsecrated mood he witnesses the Transubstantiation? " Such was their feeling as they looked down from the life that takes its course between death and a new birth: " Christ is no longer being recognised in His true being; the sacred ceremony is no longer understood."

Such feelings poured themselves out within the souls whom I have now been describing. Moreover they looked down upon that which became a sacred symbol in the reading of the Mass, the so-called Sanctissimum wherein the Host is carried on a crescent cup. It is a living symbol of the fact that once upon a time the great Sun-Being was looked for in the Christ. For the very rays of the Sun are represented on every Sanctissimum, on every Monstrance. But the connection of the Christ with the Sun had been lost. Only in the symbol was it preserved; and in the symbol it has remained until this day. Yet even in the symbol it was not understood, nor is it understood to-day. This was the second feeling that sprang forth in their souls, intensifying their sense of the need for a new Christ-experience that was to come.

In the next lecture, the day after tomorrow, we will continue to speak of the karma of the Anthroposophical Society.

VI

The School of Chartres

Among the spiritual conditions of evolution that have led to the Anthroposophical Movement and that are contained within its karma from the spiritual side, I have mentioned two external symptoms. The one is expressed in the rise of the Catechism with its questions and answers, leading towards a faith which is no longer in direct touch with the spiritual world. The other is represented by the Mass becoming exoteric. The Mass in its totality, including the Transubstantiation and Holy Communion, was made accessible to all, even to the unprepared. It thus lost its character of an ancient Mystery.

These two earthly events led those who observed them from the spiritual world to prepare in a very definite way, within the stream of spiritual evolution, for what was to become a spiritual revelation at the turn of the 19th and 20th centuries,—a revelation fitly adapted to the course of time. For this new spiritual revelation had to come after the Michael event, and in the time when the old, dark Age of Kali Yuga had run its course and a new Age was to arise for humanity. To-day we have a third thing to add. We must first bring before our souls these three spiritual conditions, which were able to draw together a number of human beings even before they descended into the physical world in the last third of the 19th or at the turn of the 19th and 20th centuries. For only when we are aware of these conditions, shall we be able to understand certain extra-karmic events which flowed into the streams of life that are welded together in the Anthroposophical Movement.

The peculiar attitude to Nature on the one hand and to

things spiritual on the other, which has evolved so greatly by our time, comes down to us only from the period that began in the 14th (15th) century. Before that time, the relationship of mankind especially to the things of the Spirit was very different. Man approached the Spirit not in concepts and ideas but in living experiences that still penetrated to the Spiritual, however slightly.

We to-day, when we speak of Nature, have a dead abstraction—empty of all being. And when we speak of the Spirit, we have something vague whose existence we presume somehow or other in the world, and comprise it in abstract concepts or ideas. It was not so in the time when the souls who are now finding their way together in the longing for a new Spirituality, had their important former incarnation, —when in that incarnation they harkened to what Initiates and Leaders of Mankind had to tell them for their inner needs. To begin with we have the age that goes on into the 7th or 8th century, when we still find a delicate connection of the human soul with the spiritual world—a conscious experience of the spiritual world itself. Even the men of knowledge and learning in that time were still in a living relationship to the spiritual world. Then we have the age beginning in the 7th or 8th century and going on to the great turning point in the 14th and 15th,—the time when the human souls who had lived in the first Christian centuries, partaking in that former period upon the earth, were once more in the life between death and a new birth.

But though—from the 6th, 7th or 8th century onwards —there was no direct connection with the spiritual world, nevertheless a certain awareness of this connection still found a haven of refuge, if I may put it so, in isolated centres of learning. In isolated centres of learning men still spoke, in knowledge, in the way they had spoken in the first Christian centuries. Nay more, it was possible for single, chosen human beings to receive deep inner impulses from the way in which the spiritual world was spoken of,— impulses enabling them, at certain times at least, to break through into the spiritual world. There were indeed isolated centres where teachings were given in a manner of which the people of to-day can have no conception.

This only came to an end in the 12th, 13th century, when at length it all flowed into a great poem in which it found as it were its consummation for the experience of mankind. I mean the Divina Commedia of Dante.

In all that lies behind the origin of the Commedia we have a wonderful chapter of human evolution. For at this moment the influences from the earth and from the cosmos are found in perpetual interplay. The two were ever flowing into one another. Human beings on the earth had lost, to some extent, the connection with the spiritual world. And in those who lived above—who, while on earth, had still experienced such a connection,—the earthly conditions which they now beheld called forth a strangely painful feeling. They saw the slow death of what they themselves had still experienced on earth. Then from the supersensible world they enthused—inspired—inspirited—certain individualities in the world of sense, so that here or there at any rate there might arise a home and centre for the real connection of man with the spiritual world.

Let us clearly bear in mind what I indicated here many years ago. Even until the 7th or 8th century—in a kind of echo of pre-Christian Initiation—Christianity was taught in centres that had remained as the high places of knowledge, relics of the ancient Mysteries. In those centres human beings were prepared, not so much by way of instruction, but by an education towards the Spirit—a training both bodily and spiritual. They were prepared for the moment when they might have at least a delicate vision of the spirituality that can manifest itself in the environment of man on earth. Then they looked outward to the realms of mineral and plant-nature and to all that lives in the animal and human kingdoms. And they saw, springing forth like an aura and fertilised in turn out of the cosmos, the spiritual-elemental beings that lived in all Nature.

Then above all there appeared to them as a living Being, whom they addressed as they would address a human being—only it was a being of a higher kind,—the Goddess Natura. She was the Goddess whom they saw before them in her full radiance, in full reality of soul. They did not speak of abstract laws of Nature, they spoke of the creative power of the Goddess Natura, working creatively in all external Nature.

She was the metamorphosis of Proserpine of antiquity. She was the ever-creating Goddess with whom he who would seek for knowledge must in a certain way unite himself. She appeared to him—appeared to him from every mineral, from every plant, from every creeping beast, from the clouds, the mountains, the river-springs. Of this Goddess who alternately in winter and in summer creates above the earth and beneath,—of this Goddess they felt: She is the hand-maid of that Divinity of whom the Gospels tell. She it is who fulfils the divine behests.

And when the seeker after knowledge had been sufficiently instructed by the Goddess about the mineral and plant and animal natures, when he was introduced into the living forces, then he learned to know from her the nature of the four Elements:—Earth, Water, Air and Fire. He learned to know the waving and weaving within the mineral and animal and plant kingdoms of the four Elements which pour themselves in all reality throughout the world:—Earth, Water, Fire, Air. He felt himself with his etheric body interwoven with the life of Earth in its gravity, Water in its life-giving power, Air in its power to awaken sentient consciousness, Fire in its power to kindle the flame of the I. In all this he felt his human being interwoven, and he felt: This was the gift of instruction from the Goddess Natura—the successor, the metamorphosis of Proserpine. The teachers saw to it that their disciples should gain a feeling, an idea of this living intercourse with Nature—Nature filled with divine forces, filled with divine substance. They saw to it that their pupils should penetrate to the living and weaving of the Elements.

Then when they had reached this point, they were introduced to the planetary system. They learnt how with the knowledge of the planetary system there arises at the same time the knowledge of the human soul. "Learn to know how the wandering stars hold sway in the heavens, and thou shalt know how thine own soul works and weaves and lives within thee." This was placed before the pupils. And at length they were led to approach what was called "The Great Ocean,"—but it was the Cosmic Ocean, which leads from the planets, from the wandering stars, to the fixed stars. Thus at length they penetrated into the secrets of the I, by learning the secrets of the universe of the fixed stars.

Mankind to-day has forgotten that such instructions were ever given; but they were. A living knowledge of this kind was cultivated until the 7th or 8th century in the last relics of the ancient Mysteries. And as a doctrine—as a theory—it was still cultivated even until that turn of the 14th and 15th centuries of which we have so often spoken. In certain centres we still see these old teachings cultivated, though with the greatest imaginable difficulties. They were well-nigh shadowed-down to concepts and ideas; yet the concepts and ideas were still living enough to kindle, in one man and another, the upward vision of all the realities of which I spoke just now.

In the 11th and especially the 12th century, reaching on to the 13th, a truly wonderful School existed. In this School there were teachers who still knew how the pupils in preceding centuries had been led to a conscious experience of the Spirit. It was the great School of Chartres. Here there flowed together all the conceptions that had issued from the living spiritual life which I have described.

Wonderful masterpieces of architecture are to be seen in Chartres to this day. Thither there had come above all a ray of the still living wisdom of Peter of Compostella, who had worked in Spain. He had cultivated a living exemplary Christianity, speaking still of Natura the handmaid of Christ, and describing still how when great Nature has introduced man to the elements, to the planetary world, to the world of stars, then and then only does he become ripe to make acquaintance in very reality of soul with the seven helpmates, who come before the human soul, not in abstract chapters of theory, but as the living Goddesses: Grammatica, Dialectica, Rhetorica, Arithmetica, Geometria, Astronomia, Musica. The pupils learned to know them as Divine-spiritual figures, living and real.

Those who were around Peter of Compostella spoke of them still as living figures. His teachings radiated into the School of Chartres. In the same School of Chartres there lived, for example, the great Bernard of Chartres, who inspired his pupils, for though he could no longer show them the Goddess Natura, nor the Goddesses of the seven Liberal Arts, still he spoke of these in so living a way that their imagined pictures at least were conjured before his pupils.

There taught Bernardus Silvestris, raising before his pupils in mighty and powerful descriptions what had been the ancient wisdom.

And above all there was John of Chartres who spoke of the human soul with an inspiration truly majestic. It was here that John of Chartres, also known as John of Salisbury, unfolded the conceptions wherein he dealt with Aristotle, —Aristotelianism. His chosen pupils were so influenced that they arrived at a new insight. They saw that such teaching as had existed in the first centuries of Christendom could no longer exist on earth, for earthly evolution could no longer bear it. It was made clear to them:—There was an ancient, almost clairvoyant knowledge, but it grew darkened. *We* can only *know* of Dialectic, Rhetoric, Astronomy, Astrology—we can no longer *behold* the Goddesses of the seven Liberal Arts.

Henceforth Aristotle must work,—Aristotle who already in antiquity was equal to the concepts and ideas of the fifth Post-Atlantean epoch.

With an inspiring force, what had thus been taught in the School of Chartres was then transplanted to the Order of Cluny, where it was turned to a more worldly form in the ecclesiastical enactments of the Abbot Hildebrand—Abbot of the Monks of Cluny—who afterwards became Pope under the name of Gregory the Seventh.

Meanwhile in the School of Chartres itself these teachings continued to be given with remarkable purity. The whole of the 12th century was radiant with them. And there was one who was in reality greater than all the others,—who taught in Chartres, with what I would call a true inspiration of ideas, the Mysteries of the seven Liberal Arts in their connection with Christianity. I mean Alain de Lille, Alanus ab Insulis. Alain de Lille at Chartres in the 12th century fired his pupils with a true enthusiasm. His great insight showed him that in the coming centuries it would no longer be possible to endow the earth with spiritual teachings such as these. For these teachings were not only Platonism; they contained the teachings from the old seership of the pre-Platonic Mysteries, with the difference that it had since received Christianity into itself.

To those in whom he presumed an understanding for such things, Alain de Lille taught already in his life-time that an Aristotelian form of knowledge would now have to work for awhile on earth,—Aristotelianism with its sharply defined conceptions and ideas. For in this way alone would it be possible to prepare for what must come again as a Spirituality in later time.

To many a human being of to-day who reads the literature of that time, it appears dull and dry. But it is by no means dry, when we gain some conception of what stood before the souls of those who taught and worked in Chartres.

And in the poetry too, which went out from Chartres, how vitally do we feel the sense of union with the living Goddesses of the seven Liberal Arts. In the poem 'Bataille des Sept Arts,' deeply penetrating as it is for anyone who understands it, we feel the living spiritual breath of the seven Liberal Arts. All these things were working in the 12th century.

You see, all this was living in the spiritual atmosphere of that time, and was still making itself felt. It was still to some extent akin to the Schools that continued to exist in Northern Italy, in Italy generally, and in Spain, though their existence was sporadic. Nevertheless these things became transplanted in a living way into all manner of spiritual currents on the earth. Towards the end of the 12th century much of this was still working at the University of Orleans, where remarkable teachings of this kind were cultivated, and something was still present of an inspiration from the School of Chartres.

And then, one day down in Italy, an Ambassador who had been in Spain, standing at that moment under a great historic impression, received a kind of sun-stroke, and there arose in him as a great and mighty revelation all that he had received as a preparatory training in his School. All this became a mighty revelation under the influence of the slight sun-stroke which came over him. Then he saw what man could see under the influence of the living principle of knowledge: He saw a mountain mightily arising with all that lived and sprang forth from it, minerals, plants, and animals, and there appeared to him the Goddess Natura, there appeared the Elements, there appeared the Planets, there appeared the Goddesses of the seven Liberal Arts, and at length Ovid as his guide and teacher. Here once again there stood before a human soul the mighty vision that had stood before the souls of men so often in the first centuries of Christianity. Such was the vision of Brunetto Latini which was afterwards handed down to Dante and from which Dante's Divina Commedia took its source.

But there was still another outcome for all those who had worked in Chartres, when they passed again through the gate of death, and, having passed through the gate of death, entered the spiritual world. Deeply significant was the spiritual life which they had led: Peter of Compostella, Bernard of Chartres, Bernardus Sylvestris, John of Chartres (John of Salisbury), Henri d'Andeli, author of the poem "Bataille des Sept Arts," and above all, Alain de Lille. Alain de Lille, in his own style of course, had written the book *Contra Hereticos,* where on behalf of Christianity he turned against the heretics, writing directly out of the old vision which was in fact the vision of the spiritual world. And now, all these souls, these individualities who had been the very last to work within the echoes of seership, the wisdom seen in fulness of spiritual light,—they all of them entered into the spiritual world. And in that spiritual world they came together with other souls, of great significance, who were preparing for a new earthly life just at that time. For they were preparing to descend in the very near future into an earthly life where they would work in the sense that was necessary, to bring about the subsequent turning-point: the turning-point of the 14th and 15th century. We have a great spiritual life before us, my dear friends. The last great ones of the School of Chartres had just arrived in the spiritual world. Those individualities who afterwards brought forth the full flower of Scholasticism were still there in the spiritual world, and at the beginning of the 13th century there took place one of the most important exchanges of ideas behind the scenes of human evolution,—an exchange of ideas between those who had carried up the old Platonism, inspired by spiritual vision, from the School of Chartres into the supersensible world, and those on the other hand who were preparing to carry Aristotelianism down to earth, as the great transition to bring about a new Spirituality that was to flow into the evolution of mankind in the future.

They came to an agreement with one another. The individualities from the School of Chartres spoke, as it were, to those who were preparing to descend into the physical world of sense, who were preparing to cultivate Aristotelianism in the Scholastic system which was right for that age. They spoke to them as it were, and said: For us it is impossible to work on earth for the present; for the earth is not now in a condition to cultivate knowledge in this living way. What we, the last bearers of Platonism, were still able to cultivate must now give place to Aristotelianism. We will remain up here.

Thus the great spirits of Chartres remained in the supersensible world, nor have they returned hitherto in any earthly incarnations of significance. But they were working mightily, helping in the formation of that mighty Imagination in the spiritual world that was formed in the first half of the 19th century and of which I have already told you. They worked in full harmony with those who descended with their Aristotelianism to the earth.

The Dominican Order, above all, contained individualities who lived in this kind of " supersensible contract," if I may so describe it, with the great spirits of Chartres, for they had agreed with them: " We will descend in order to continue the cultivation of knowledge in the Aristotelian form. You will remain up here. On earth too we shall remain in union with you. Platonism for the present cannot prosper on the earth. We shall find you again when we return, and then together we will prepare for that time when the period of Scholastic Aristotelianism will have been completed in earthly evolution, and it will be possible to unfold Spirituality once more in communion with you, with the spirits of Chartres."

It was, for example, an event of deep significance when Alain de Lille, as he had been called in earthly life, sent down to earth a pupil well instructed by him in the spiritual world. For in this pupil he sent down on to the earth all the discrepancies, it is true, which could arise between Platonism and Aristotelianism, but he sent them down so that they might be harmonised through the Scholastic principle of that time. Such was the spiritual working, especially in the 13th century, to the end that there might flow together the workings of those who were on the earth,—who were on the earth for instance in the garment of Dominicans,—and those who had remained in yonder world. For the time being, these latter could find no earthly bodies in which to stamp their spirituality. For theirs was a spirituality which could not come down to the Aristotelian element.

So there arose in the 13th century a wonderful co-operation of that which was being done on earth with that which was flowing down from above. Often those who were on earth were not conscious of this working from the other side, but those who were working on the other side were all the more conscious. It was a truly living co-operation. One would say, the principle of the Mysteries had ascended to the heavens and sent down its Sun-rays thence upon all that was working on the earth.

This went into all the details and can be traced above all in the detailed things that happened. Alain de Lille, in his own earthly life as a teacher at Chartres, had only been able to go so far that at a certain age of life he put on the garment of the Cistercians. He became a priest of the Cistercian Order. In the Cistercian Order at that time, in the exercises of that Order, the last relics of a striving to awaken Platonism—the Platonic world-conception, in unison with Christianity—had found a refuge.

The way in which he sent a pupil down to the earth expressed itself in this: he sent his pupil down to continue through the Dominican Order the task that was now to pass over to Aristotelianism.

The transition expressed itself outwardly in a remarkable symptom. For the pupil of Alanus ab Insulis of whom I am speaking,—his pupil, that is to say, in the worlds above the earth,—having descended to the earth, first wore the garment of a Cistercian, which he only afterwards exchanged for that of a Dominican.

Such were the individualities who worked together: those who afterwards became the leading Schoolmen and their pupils,—human souls long connected with one another, —and these in turn united with the great spirits of the School of Chartres, united in the sensible and supersensible worlds during the 13th and on into the early 14th century.

Such was the mighty world-historic plan. Those who could not descend to Aristotelianism upon the earth remained in the spiritual world above, waiting until the purposes in which they were all so intimately united should have been carried forward by the others upon the earth, under the influence of the sharply outlined concepts and ideas proceeding from Aristotelianism.

It was really like a conversation upward and downward from the spiritual to the earthly world, from the earthly to the spiritual world, in that 13th century.

Indeed it was only into this spiritual atmosphere that true Rosicrucianism was able to pour its influence.

When those who had descended to the earth to give the impulse of Aristotelianism had accomplished their task, they too were lifted into the spiritual world and went on working there: Platonists and Aristotelians together. And now there came and gathered round them the souls of whom I have already spoken to you—the souls of the two groups I mentioned.

Thus we find entering into the karma of the Anthroposophical Movement a large number of disciples of Chartres. Entering into this discipleship of Chartres we find the souls who had come from one or other of the two streams of which I spoke here in the last few days. It is a large circle of human beings, for many are living in this circle who have not as yet found their way to the Anthroposophical Movement. Nevertheless it is so: what we find in the field of Anthroposophy to-day has been prepared for through these manifold experiences.

A remarkable influence came over the Cistercian Order for example, when Alain de Lille, Alanus ab Insulis, put on the garment of a Cistercian—when he with his Platonism became a Cistercian Priest. Indeed this element never left the Cistercian Order. In relation to these things which we must now unveil, I may perhaps be allowed a few personal observations that could not be included in my autobiography. There was a circumstance in my life which was destined to lead me to the knowledge of many an inner connection in this domain, (other connections were revealed to me from different quarters). I was led to many things through the circumstance that in my life, before the Weimar period, I could never escape from the presence, in one way or another, of the Cistercian Order; and yet again I was always somehow kept at a distance from it. I grew up, so to speak, in the shadow of the Cistercian Order, which has important settlements in the neighbourhood of Wiener-Neustadt. Those who had to educate most of the youth in the district where I grew up, were Priests of the Cistercian

Order. I had the robe of this Order perpetually before me, the white robe with the black band around the waist, or, as we call it, the stola. Had I had occasion to speak of such things in my autobiography I could have said: Everything in my life tended in the direction of a classical education at the *Gymnasium* and not of that modern education which I actually underwent in the *Real-Schule* in Wiener-Neustadt. Now the *Gymnasium* in that place was at that time still in the hands of the Cistercians. It was a strange play of forces that drew me to them and at the same time held me at a distance.

Again, the whole circle of monks in the Theological Faculty at the University of Vienna,—the circle around Marie Eugenie delle Grazie,—consisted of Cistercians. With these Cistercians I had the most intimate theological conversations—the most intimate conversations on Christology. I only indicate this fact, seeing that it enters into my perception of that period of the 12th century, when the flower of the School of Chartres poured its life into the Cistercian Order. For indeed, in the peculiarly attractive scholarship of the Cistercians there lived on—albeit in a corrupted way—something of the magic of the School of Chartres. Important and manifold enquiries were pursued by Cistercians whom I knew well. And to me those things were most important which revealed to me: It is indeed impossible for any of those who were the disciples of Chartres to incarnate at present, and yet it seems as though some of the individualities connected with that School became incorporated, if I may call it so, for brief periods, in some of the human beings who wore the Cistercian garment.

Separated, if I may put it so, by a thin wall only, there ever continued to work on the earth what was being prepared as I have described it, in supersensible worlds, leading to that great preparation in the first half of the 19th century.

And for me it was a highly remarkable experience to have that conversation to which I referred in my autobiography,—that conversation on the Christ Being with a Priest of the Cistercian Order, which took place not in delle Grazie's house but as we were going away from her house together. For the conversation was carried on, not from the present-day dogmatic standpoint of Theology, but from the standpoint of Neo-Scholasticism. It went with full depth into the things that had once existed upon the earth, with Aristotelian clarity and definition of concept, and yet at the same time with Platonic spiritual light.

That which was to arise in Anthroposophy shone through already, though in secret and mysterious ways, through the events of the time. Though indeed it could not shine through into human souls where they were harnessed to one religious or social group or another, nevertheless it shone through, through the connections which certain human souls still had with the great spiritual currents that do, after all, work upon the earth.

Between the beginning of the Michael Age and the end of the Kali Yuga, it was indeed possible to recognise, in much that was working in individual human beings in the most varied domains of life, the language of the Spirit of the Time. For the speaking of the Spirit of the Time was a great call for the anthroposophical revelations to come. We saw the living rise of Anthroposophy, as of a being that was to be born but that was still resting in a mother's womb. For it was resting in the womb of preparation, that had worked from the first Christian centuries towards the School of Chartres, then to be continued in supersensible spheres, in cooperation with what was here on the earth, in the Aristotelian defence of Christianity. It was out of these impulses, as we find them expressed in Alain de Lille's work *Contra Hereticos*, that there afterwards arose such a work as the *Summa Fidei Catholicae contra Gentiles* of Thomas Aquinas. And there arose that characteristic feature of the time which speaks to us from all the pictures, where we see the Dominican Doctors of the Church treading Averroes, Avicenna and the others under foot. For this indicates the living and spirited defence of spiritual Christianity, and yet withal the transition to intellectualism.

My dear friends, I cannot describe this world of facts in any theoretic way; for by theorising, these things are weakened and made pale. *Facts* I wanted to place before your souls,—facts from which you will feel whereto your gaze must be directed if you would see those souls, who passed before their present earthly life through a spiritual experience between death and a new birth, in such a way that when on the earth, they longed for Anthroposophy.

The most divergent, the most opposite conceptions work together in the world, weaving a living whole.

And to-day, those who were working in the great School of Chartres in the 12th century, and those who were united with them at the beginning of the 13th century in one of the greatest spiritual communities,—albeit in the supersensible world—to-day again they are working together. The great spirits of Chartres are working with those, who in unison with them subsequently cultivated Aristotelianism on the earth. It matters not, that some of them are working here on the earth, while others cannot yet descend to the earth. They are working together now, intending a new spiritual epoch in earthly evolution. And their great purpose now, is to collect the souls who for a long time have been united with them,—to gather together the souls with whose help a new spiritual age can then be founded. Their purpose is, in one way or another and within a comparatively short time, in the midst of an otherwise decadent civilization, to make possible a renewed cooperation in earthly life between the spirits of Chartres from the 12th century and the spirits of the 13th century who are united with them. Their purpose is to prepare, so that they will be able to work together in an earthly life, cultivating spirituality once more within the civilization which, apart from this, is sailing on into destruction and disintegration.

Intentions that are being cherished to-day, not upon earth but as between earth and heaven, such intentions I have wanted to explain to you. Enter deeply into all that lies in these intentions, and you will feel, as a living influence upon your souls, the spiritual background, of which the necessary foreground is the streaming together of human souls in this Anthroposophical Movement.

VII

The New Age of Michael

We have traced the events in the physical and superphysical worlds which underlie what is now striving to make itself known to the world in Anthroposophy. We know, my dear friends, that in the last few decades two very important incisions have occurred,—important for the whole evolution of mankind. There is the one to which I have so often drawn attention, I mean the end of the so-called Dark Age at the turn of the 19th and 20th centuries. An age of light has now begun as against the preceding age of darkness. We know that the age of darkness led eventually to that condition of the human soul which closed the spiritual eyes of man completely to the supersensible world. We know that in ancient times of human evolution it was a common condition of mankind to see into the spiritual world, albeit in a dream-like and more or less instinctive way. To doubt the reality of the spiritual world was utterly impossible in olden times of human evolution. But if that old condition had continued—if mankind had lived on in that instinctive vision of the spiritual world—there would never have arisen in human evolution what we may call the Intelligence of the individual human being, the manipulation of the intellect or reasoning faculty by the individual, personal man. And this, as we know, is connected with that which leads the human being to freedom of will. The one is unthinkable without the other. Thus in that dim, instinctive condition which once belonged to mankind, wherein they experienced the ever-present spiritual world, man could not attain to freedom, nor could he attain to that independent Thinking which we may call: the use of Intelligence by the single human individual.

The time had to come for these two things: The free and personal use of Intelligence, and the freedom of the human Will. Hence for human consciousness the original, instinctive vision that penetrated to the spiritual world had to disappear. All this has now been accomplished. Though it is not quite clear to every single man, yet it has been accomplished for mankind in general. With the close of the 19th century, the dark age—the age that darkened the spiritual world, yet at the same time opened up the use of Intelligence and of Free Will to man—had run its course. We are now entering upon an age when man must once again be touched—in the ways that are possible—touched by the spiritual world in its reality.

True, we cannot say that this age has begun in a very light-filled way. It is as though the first decades of the 20th century had brought over humanity all the evil that mankind has ever experienced in the course of history. And yet in spite of this, the possibility has come into the general course of human evolution, to reach the light of spiritual life. It is only by a kind of inertia that men have persisted in the habits of the age of darkness. They have carried these habits on into the 20th century; and just because the light can now arise, illumining the truth, these habits of the age of darkness have come forth in a far more evil form than was possible in the Kali-Yuga when they were justified.

Now we also know that this direction of all humanity towards a new age of light was prepared for through the fact that at the end of the 1870's the Age of Michael began. Let us place again before our souls what it means to say that the Age of Michael began with the last third of the 19th century.

We know that as we are surrounded here by the three kingdoms of outer Nature, the mineral, plant and animal kingdoms in the physical world of sense, so we are surrounded in the spiritual world by the higher kingdoms of which we have spoken in so many connections as the kingdoms of the Hierarchies. Even as we descend into the kingdoms of Nature, beginning with man and coming down to the animal kingdom, so, as we ascend to the supersensible, we come to the kingdom of the Angeloi. The Angels have the task of guiding and protecting the individual human being as he passes from earthly life to earthly life. Thus the tasks that fall to the spiritual world in relation to the individual human being, are allotted to the Beings of the kingdom of Angeloi.

We then go on up to the kingdom of Archangeloi, who have the most varied tasks. Now it is one of their tasks to guide and direct the fundamental tendencies of successive ages in relation to man.

Thus for about three centuries before the end of the eighteen-seventies, there was what we may call the dominion of Gabriel. For one who studies the evolution of humanity, not on the surface as is customary to-day, but in the depths, this dominion of Gabriel is expressed in the fact that the deepest and most important impulses in the process of humanity during that time were implanted in those forces which we may call the forces of heredity. Never were the forces of physical inheritance that work through the generations so important as in the three centuries preceding the last third of the 19th century.

Let us see, my dear friends, how this expresses itself. We know that in the 19th century the problem of heredity became the most pressing and important in the consciousness of men. Man felt how his qualities of soul and spirit are dependent on heredity. It was as though at the last moment he came to feel what had been holding sway in human evolution as a real Law of Nature in the 16th, 17th, and 18th, and in a great part of the 19th century.

During that time it was so indeed: man carried even into his spiritual development the qualities he had inherited from his parents and ancestors. During that time those qualities became especially important which are connected with physical reproduction. Again we find an outward sign of this fact in the great interest which was felt at the end of the 19th century in the question of reproduction and indeed in all sexual questions. In the centuries to which I have just referred, the most important spiritual impulses had approached humanity in this way, they had sought for realisation through physical inheritance.

Now the age in which Michael leads and guides humanity will stand in complete contrast to all this. I mean, therefore, the age that began at the end of the seventies of the last century,—the age in which we are, and the impulses of which are interwoven with what we are also learning to know as the new Age of Light beginning in the 20th century. For the streams of these two impulses work together.

To-day we will dwell upon this question: What is the characteristic feature of an Age of Michael? I say, of *an* Age of Michael. For the spiritual guidance and leadership to which I have just referred is as follows. It is always so: one of the Beings of the kingdom of Archangeloi has the spiritual leadership in human evolution for about three centuries, in that region where civilisation is predominantly taking place.

Gabriel, as I said, had the leadership in the 16th, 17th, 18th and 19th centuries. His place is now taken by Michael. There are seven of these Archangels who lead humanity, and thus the several guidances of the Archangeloi recur in cyclic order. We to-day, who live in an Age of Michael, have every reason to call to mind the last Age of Michael which happened in the spiritual guidance of mankind.

The last Age of Michael preceded the founding of Christianity, preceded the Mystery of Golgotha. It came to an end in ancient times approximately with the deeds of Alexander and with the founding of the philosophy of Aristotle.

If we follow out all that took place in ancient Greece and the surrounding countries for about three hundred years before the time of Alexander the Great and Aristotle, we find ourselves once more in an Age of Michael. An Age of Michael is characterised by many different conditions, but especially by this, that in such an age the most spiritual interests of humanity (according to the particular disposition of the time) become predominant. In such an age especially, a cosmopolitan, international character will permeate the world. National distinctions cease.

Now it was above all in the Age of Gabriel that the national impulses within European civilisation, with its American appendage, became so firmly rooted. In our Age of Michael, in the course of the next three centuries, these national impulses will be completely overcome. This is the case in every Age of Michael: a common feature runs through all humanity—something of an all-human character, as against the special interests of single groups or nations.

In the last age of Michael's dominion on the earth, before the Mystery of Golgotha, it found the following expression. Out of the conditions that had taken shape in ancient Greece there arose that mighty historic tendency which led eventually to the campaigns of Alexander. In the campaigns of Alexander, Grecian culture and civilisation was carried, with extraordinary genius, right into Asia and Africa, and spread through many nations and peoples who until then had adhered to quite different things. This stupendous deed found its culmination in what was then founded in Alexandria. It was a great cosmopolitan movement, seeking to give to the whole of the then civilised world the spiritual forces that had gathered on the soil of ancient Greece. Such are the things that happen under the impulse of Michael, and that happened then too under his impulse.

Now those who took part in these earthly deeds, done in the service of Michael, were no longer upon the earth during the time of the Mystery of Golgotha. All the beings who belonged to the realm of Michael—no matter whether they were disembodied human souls, transplanted by death into the spiritual world when the Michael Age had run its course, or whether they were souls who never incarnated upon the earth—they all were united in a common life within the supersensible world, in the time when upon the earth the Mystery of Golgotha was taking place.

We must make fully present to our heart and mind the facts that lie before us here. If we choose the aspect of the earth, my dear friends, if this earth is our standpoint, then we say: Humanity on the earth reaches a certain point in earthly evolution. Christ, the lofty Spirit of the Sun, is arriving on the earth, incarnating in the human being Jesus of Nazareth. Those who dwell on the earth experience the fact that Christ, the great Spirit of the Sun, arrives among them. But they have little knowledge that could really cause them to understand the greatness of the stupendous and unique event.

All the more knowledge have those disembodied souls who are gathered around Michael and who are living in the realm of the Sun-existence in worlds above the earth. All the more do they know how to value what is taking place, as they witness it from their different aspect. These souls witnessed what was then taking place for the World, from the Sun. Christ who had hitherto worked within the realm of the Sun, who had only been attainable in the Mysteries when they ascended to the Sun-existence—Christ now departed from the Sun to unite Himself with earthly humanity upon the earth. This was what they witnessed.

It was a mighty and awe-inspiring event, above all for those who belonged to the communion of Michael. For, those who belong to the communion of Michael have a peculiar connection with all that represents the cosmic destinies proceeding from the Sun. They had to take their leave of Christ, who until then had had His dwelling-place in the Sun and was thenceforth to take His place on the earth. This is the other aspect.

But there was another thing connected with it, which we can only rightly understand if we take the following into account. To think—to live in thoughts that spring forth from within—as we do to-day, was impossible for the men of ancient times. They might be wise, indeed infinitely wiser than modern humanity, but they were not ‘ clever ’ in the sense of cleverness to-day. To-day we call a man clever who is able to produce thoughts out of himself, who is able to think logically—to bring one thought into connection with another, and so forth. In olden times there was no such thing—no such thing as Thoughts independently produced. The Thoughts were sent down to the earth at one and the same time with the Revelations that came to man from the spiritual world. Man did not think and ponder, but he received the spiritual content by Revelation, and he received it in such a way that the Thoughts came with it. To-day we think and ponder about things. In those ancient times the impressions which the souls received brought the Thoughts with them. The Thoughts were inspired, not self-made Thoughts. Now he who ordered the Cosmic Intelligence which thus came to man along with the spiritual Revelations—he who ordered this Cosmic Intelligence, who had, so to speak, dominion over it,—is the same spiritual Being whom we, when we make use of our Christian terminology, call the Archangel Michael. He had to administer the Cosmic Intelligence in the cosmos.

We must make clear to ourselves what this really means. It is a fact that such human beings as Alexander the Great, though in a somewhat different context of ideas, had a distinct consciousness of the fact that their thoughts came to them by way of Michael. True, the spiritual Being whom we mean, was called by a different name. We are making use of the Christian terminology, but it is not the terminology that matters. Such a man as Alexander the Great regarded himself as none other than a Missionary of Michael, an instrument of Michael. He could think in no other way than this: Michael is acting on the earth, and I am the instrument through which he acts. Such was the conception, and this gave him the strength of will in deed and action. Nor did a thinker in that time think differently than thus, that Michael was working in him and giving him the thoughts.

Now this too was connected with the descent of Christ to the earth: Michael and his hosts witnessed not only the departure of Christ from the Sun, but above all they saw how Michael himself was gradually losing his dominion over the Cosmic Intelligence. Quite distinctly they saw from the Sun that revelations would no longer come to men from the spiritual world with the content of Intelligence. They saw that the time must come when man himself must reach his own intelligence on the earth. It was a significant and incisive event to see the Intelligence pouring down, as it were, to the earth. By and by, I if may use this expression, the Intelligence was no longer to be found in the heavens; it was let down to earth.

This was fulfilled especially in the first Christian centuries. In the earliest Christian centuries we still see those human beings who were capable of it, having at least a few glimpses of what was flowing to them with the content of Intelligence as revelations from beyond the earth. This went on even into the 8th or 9th century A.D. Then came the great moment of decision. It came in such a way that Michael and those who belonged to him, no matter whether incarnate or discarnate, must say to themselves: " Men upon earth are beginning to become intelligent themselves—beginning to bring forth their own power of understanding from within them. The Cosmic Intelligence can no longer be administered by Michael." Michael felt that the dominion over the Cosmic Intelligence was passing from him—falling from his grasp. While down below—looking down on to the earth—they saw this new age of Intelligence, beginning from the 8th or 9th century onwards. Men were beginning to form their own thoughts for themselves.

I have already described, my dear friends, how in certain special Schools—for instance in the great School of Chartres, —they handed down the traditions of what had once been revealed to men, steeped in the Cosmic Intelligence. I described to you how much was achieved in the School of Chartres, especially in the 12th century; and I tried to indicate how the administration of Intelligence on the earth literally passed over to individual members especially of the Dominican Order. We need only look into the works that arose out of Christian Scholasticism—that wonderful spiritual stream which is so entirely misunderstood to-day, by its supporters no less then by its opponents, because they do not observe its really important feature. We need only look into these Scholastic works and see how they wrestled to understand what is the real and deep significance of Concepts—of the content of Intelligence—for mankind and for the things of the world. The great conflict between

Nominalism and Realism was developed especially in the Dominican Order. The ' Nominalist ' sees no more than names in general concepts. The ' Realist ' sees in them real spiritual content, made manifest in the things of the world. The whole of Scholasticism is a wrestling of mankind for a clear understanding of the Intelligence that is pouring in. No wonder that the main interest of those around Michael was directed above all to what was unfolding upon the earth in this Christian Scholasticism. In all that St. Thomas Aquinas and his pupils, and many other Schoolmen, were bringing forth, we see the earthly stamp and impress of the Michael stream of that time—the Michael stream, the administration of Intelligence, of the light-filled Spiritual Intelligence.

And now the Intelligence was here on earth. Now man had to strive for clarity as to its meaning. Looking down from the spiritual world, on to the earth, one could see how that which had belonged to the realm of Michael was now unfolding down below, outside of his dominion, for it was unfolding in the beginning of the dominion of Gabriel.

The Wisdom of Initiation—the Rosicrucian wisdom which was going forth at that time—consisted in this, that one had a certain clarity of understanding for these facts.

Especially in that time of history it is important to see how the earthly and the supersensible are connected. Outwardly the earthly life looks as though it had been loosened, cut off from the supersensible,—and yet it is connected. You can see how it is connected from what I described in our last lectures.

The supersensible facts that here follow, can only be described in pictures, in Imaginations. They cannot be put into abstract concepts. They must be livingly described. Therefore I must now describe what happened in the beginning of the age when the Spiritual Soul, and with it the Intelligence, enters in and becomes a part of humanity.

Several centuries had passed since Michael, in the 9th century A.D., had seen arriving on the earth what had hitherto been the Cosmic Intelligence. He now witnessed its further course on earth. He saw it flowing onward now on earth, especially in Scholasticism. This was below. He on the other hand gathered around him those who belonged to his realm in the domain of the Sun. He gathered them all—human souls who happened to be in the life between death and a new birth, and those, also belonging to his realm, who in their own evolution never enter into human bodies yet have a certain connection with mankind. You may imagine, those human souls especially were there, whom I have mentioned as the great teachers of Chartres. Among the greatest who at that time, at the beginning of the 15th century, were in the hosts of Michael and had their deeds to do in the spiritual world,—among the greatest of them was Alanus ab Insulis. But all the others too were there, those whom I have named as belonging to the School of Chartres. United with them were the others who by now had returned to the life between death and a new birth, who had come back again from the Order of the Dominicans. Souls, therefore, belonging to the Platonic stream were intimately united with souls who belonged to the Aristotelian times. All these had experienced and undergone the several impulses of Michael. Many of them lived in such a way as to have witnessed the Mystery of Golgotha, not from the earthly aspect, but from the aspect of the Sun. And at that time, at the beginning of the 15th century, their situations in the spiritual world were fraught with peculiar significance.

Then there arose under the leadership of Michael something which we may call, as we must use earthly expressions, a supersensible School. What had once been the Michael Mystery—what had been told to the Initiates in the ancient Mysteries of Michael, and must now become different, since the Intelligence had found its way from the cosmos to the earth—all this Michael himself now gathered up, expressing it again with untold significance to those whom he had gathered around him in this School of Michael. For it was a supersensible School of Michael at the beginning of the 15th century. All that once lived as the Michael Mystery in the Sun Mysteries now became alive again in supersensible worlds. It was a wonderful summing-up of the Platonism that had been continued in the Aristotelian manner, and of all that Alexander the Great had carried into Asia and down into Egypt. It was expounded how the ancient spirituality still lived in this. In this supersensible School all the souls took part who had ever been connected with the stream of which I have now been speaking to you in many lectures. I mean the souls who are now predestined to belong to the Anthroposophical Movement,—whose karma, as it takes shape, leads them to the Anthroposophical Movement. For all that was taught in that School was taught from this point of view, that in the evolution of humanity below, the Michael principle must thenceforth be developed in a different way, namely through the Intelligence of the human soul itself.

It was pointed out how at the end of the 19th century (in the last third of this century) Michael himself would once again assume dominion upon the earth. Throughout the intervening time since the age of Alexander, the six other Archangels would have fulfilled their several dominions. Now a new Michael Age would begin. But this new Michael Age must be different from the others. For the other Ages of Michael were such that the Cosmic Intelligence had always expressed itself in the common sphere of humanity. But now,—thus said Michael in supersensible worlds to his pupils,—now in the new Michael Age something quite different would be required. For what Michael had administered for men through many aeons, pouring it into earthly existence in living inspirations, this had now fallen away from him. But he was to find it again when at the end of the seventies of the 19th century he would begin his new earthly rule. He would find it again at a time when, to begin with, an Intelligence bereft of spirituality had taken root among men. And he would find it in a peculiar condition,—most intensely exposed to the Ahrimanic forces. For in the very time when the Intelligence was descending from the cosmos to the earth, the aspirations of the Ahrimanic powers grew ever greater, striving to wrest the Cosmic Intelligence from

Michael as soon as it became earthly Intelligence, striving to make it dominant on earth alone, free of Michael.

Such was the crisis from the beginning of the 15th century until our day—the crisis in the midst of which we are, which expresses itself as the battle of Ahriman and Michael. For Ahriman is using all his power to challenge Michael's dominion over the Intelligence that has now become earthly. And Michael, with all the impulses that are his, though his dominion over the Intelligence has fallen from him, is striving to take hold of it again on earth at the beginning of his new earthly rule, from the year 1879 onwards. Human evolution stood at this decisive point in the last third of the 19th century. The Intelligence, formerly cosmic, had become earthly, and there was Ahriman, wanting to make it altogether earthly. He wants to make it continue in the way that began during the age of Gabriel, making it earthly, making it an affair only of the human communities of blood—an affair of the generations, the forces of reproduction and inheritance. All this Ahriman desires.

Michael came down towards the earth. He could alone desire to find again, on earth, what had had to take its own course in the intervening time in order that man might attain Intelligence and Freedom. He could alone desire to find it again in such a way that he might take hold of it on earth and become, within the earth once more, Lord of the Intelligence that is now working within mankind. Ahriman versus Michael: Michael finding himself obliged to defend against Ahriman what he had ruled through the aeons of time for the benefit of humankind. Mankind stands in the midst of this battle; and among other things, to be an anthroposophist is to understand this battle to a certain extent at least. It shows itself everywhere; in its true form it is there behind the scenes of the historical events, but it shows itself even in the facts that lie manifest before us.

My dear friends, those who were in that supersensible School of Michael partook in the teachings which I have outlined so very briefly. The teachings they heard were a repetition of what had been taught in the Sun Mysteries since ancient time. They were already a prophecy of what was to be achieved when the new Age of Michael began. They were an inspired call, a solemn challenge to those who are gathered around Michael, to hurl themselves into his stream and take hold of his true impulse, to the end that Intelligence may once again be united to the being of Michael.

While these wonderful teachings were going forth to the souls in that supersensible School directed by Michael himself, the same souls were taking part in an awe-inspiring event that could only appear within the evolution of our cosmos after long, long epochs of time. We on the earth, when we speak of the Divine, look up to the supersensible world. When we are in the life between death and a new birth, as I have indicated once before, we really look down on to the earth, albeit not the physical earth. As we look down on to the earth, great and mighty, divine-spiritual workings reveal themselves to us. Now at the time (at the beginning of the 15th century) when that School began, of which I said that many souls within the realm of Michael took part in it, at that very time one could witness something that is repeated in cosmic evolution after only long, long centuries. As one looked down to the earth, one witnessed, as it were how Seraphim, Cherubim and Thrones—the members of the highest Hierarchies—were accomplishing a mighty deed. It was in the first third of the 15th century, in the time when behind the scenes of modern history the Rosicrucian School was founded. Ordinarily when one looks down to the earthly realm from the life between death and a new birth, one sees the deeds of the Seraphim, Cherubim and Thrones taking place in a uniform and steady way. One sees the Seraphim, Cherubim and Thrones carrying the Spiritual from the realm of the Exusiai, Dynamis and Kyriotetes down into the Physical, and by their power implanting the Spiritual into the Physical. But, ever and again after long epochs of time, one witnesses an awe-inspiring departure from what is thus seen in the ordinary course of being. It was in the Atlantean time that such a thing had last shown itself, as seen from the aspect of the Supersensible. What is taking place at such a moment in humanity shows itself thus:—As one looks down from the spiritual world, one sees the earth in all its realms flashed through by lightning flashes; one hears a mighty, rolling thunder. It was one of the cosmic thunderstorms that take their course while human beings upon earth are as though wrapt in sleep. But it revealed itself mightily to the spirits around Michael.

Behind all that took place historically in the soul of man at the beginning of the 15th century, there stands a tremendous process which revealed itself to the pupils of Michael at the very time when they were receiving their teachings in the supersensible. In Atlantean time, when the Cosmic Intelligence, while remaining cosmic, had taken possession of the hearts of men, such an event had taken place; and now for the present earthly realm it once again broke forth in spiritual lightning and thunder. Yes, it was so indeed. In the age when men were conscious of the earthly historic convulsions only,—when the Rosicrucians were going forth, when all manner of remarkable events were happening of which you can read in external history, —in that age the earth appeared, to the spirits in the supersensible worlds, surrounded by mighty lightnings and thunderclaps. The Seraphim, Cherubim and Thrones were carrying over the Cosmic Intelligence into that member of man's organisation which we call the system of nerves and senses, the head-organisation. Once again a great event had taken place. It does not show itself distinctly as yet, it will only do so in the course of hundreds or thousands of years; but it means, my dear friends, that man is being utterly transformed. Formerly he was a heart-man; then he became a head-man. The Intelligence becomes his own. Seen from the supersensible, all this is of immense significance. All the power and strength that lies in the domain of the first Hierarchy, in the domain of the Seraphim and Cherubim who reveal their strength and power through the fact that that they not only administer the Spiritual *within* the Spiritual, like the Dynamis, Exusiai and Kyriotetes, but carry the

Spiritual into the Physical, making it a creator of the Physical,—all this their power the Seraphim, Cherubim and Thrones now had to apply in accomplishing a deed such as takes place, as I said, only after many aeons. And one might say: What Michael taught to his own during that time was heralded in the earthly worlds beneath with thunder and lightning. This should be understood, my dear friends, for these thunders and lightnings must become enthusiasm in the hearts and minds of anthroposophists. And whoever really has the impulse towards Anthroposophy—(though it be unconsciously as yet, for men do not know it yet, but they will learn it in good time)—whoever has this impulse within him, still bears in his soul the echoes, the after-echoes of the fact that in the circle of Michael he received yonder heavenly Anthroposophy. For the heavenly Anthroposophy went before the earthly. The teachings given at that time were to prepare for what is now to become Anthroposophy on the earth.

Thus we have a double supersensible preparation for what is to become Anthroposophy on the earth. We have the preparation in the great supersensible School from the 15th century onward, and then we have what I have described as an Imaginative cult or ritual (*Cultus*) that took shape in the supersensible at the end of the 18th and beginning of the 19th century, when all that the Michael pupils had learned in the supersensible School before, was cast into mighty pictures and Imaginations. Thus were the souls prepared, who afterwards descended into the physical world, being destined through all these preparations to feel the inner impulse to seek for what would work as Anthroposophy on earth.

Think of them all! The great teachers of Chartres took part. They, as you know from my last descriptions, have not yet come down again, but they sent out before them those who worked above all in the Dominican Order, having held a kind of conference with them at the turn of the 12th and 13th centuries. All these souls afterwards came together again—those who with fiery lips had declared ancient and sacred teachings in the School of Chartres, and those again who had wrestled in the cold and clear, but heart-devoted works of Scholasticism, to master the true meaning of Intelligence. All these were among the hosts of Michael, learning the lessons of the School which I have indicated.

We have this School of Michael, and we have the great Imaginative ritual at the beginning of the 19th century, of the effects of which I have also spoken. Then we have the significant fact that at the end of the eighteen-seventies the dominion of Michael began again. Michael prepares once more to receive, down here on earth, the Intelligence that fell away from him in the intervening time. Intelligence must become Michael-like again. We must understand the sense of the new Age of Michael. Those who come to-day with the inner urge to a spirituality that already shows such Intelligence within it, as in the Anthroposophical Movement, are souls who are already here at this day according to their karma, to pay heed to what is taking place on earth in the beginning of the Age of Michael. But they are connected with all those who have not yet come down again. They are connected above all with those of the Platonic stream who still remain above, in supersensible existence, under the leadership of Bernardus Silvestris, Alanus ab Insulis and the others.

Those who are able to receive Anthroposophy to-day with true and deep devotion in their hearts—those who are able to unite themselves with Anthroposophy—have within them the impulse, as a result of all they experienced in the supersensible at the beginning of the 15th century and at the beginning of the 19th century, to appear again on earth at the end of the 20th century together with the others who have not yet returned. By that time anthroposophical spirituality will have prepared for what must then be realised, through the community of them all, namely, for the fuller revelation of all that has been supersensibly prepared through the different streams that I have named.

My dear friends, the anthroposophist should receive these things into his consciousness. He should understand that he is called to prepare already now that spirituality which must expand ever more and more, till the culmination is reached at the end of the 20th century, when true anthroposophists will be able to be here again, united with the others. *Conscious* the true anthroposophist must be that the need to-day is to look with active participation and to co-operate in the battle between Ahriman and Michael. Only when a spirituality, such as is seeking to flow through the Anthroposophical Movement on earth, unites with other spiritual streams, will Michael find the impulses which will unite him once more with the Intelligence that has grown earthly but that in truth belongs to him.

It will yet be my task to show you by what refined and clever means Ahriman is seeking to hinder this, so that you will see how sharp is the conflict that rages in our 20th century. Through all these things we can become aware of the earnestness of the time and of the courage that is needed if we are to take our right place in these spiritual streams. Yet at the same time the man who truly receives these things may say to himself: " Thou human soul, if only thou understand, mayest be called to help in making sure the dominion of Michael." Then there can arise in the human soul an inner joy of devotion, a song of gladness that it is given to him to be so filled with strength. But this feeling of strong courage and courageous strength must first be found. For it stands written above us in spiritual letters: " Be conscious that you will have to return before the end and at the end of the 20th century, which you yourselves have prepared. Be conscious how it will then be able to take shape, even as you prepared it."

To know oneself in the very midst of this battle, this decisive conflict between Michael and Ahriman, is one thing, my dear friends, that lies inherent in true anthroposophical enthusiasm and inspiration.

VIII

AHRIMAN'S FIGHT AGAINST THE MICHAEL PRINCIPLE

THE MESSAGE OF MICHAEL

We shall now have to describe how the individual anthroposophist can come to experience his karma through the simple fact that he has placed himself into the Anthroposophical Society, or at any rate into the Anthroposophical Movement, through all the previous conditions of which we have already spoken. To this end it will be necessary for me to add a few explanations to what I set forth last Monday. I told you of the deeply important supersensible School at the beginning of the 15th century. To characterise it we can say: Michael himself was the great Teacher in that School. Numbers of souls, human souls who were then in the life between death and a new birth, and numbers too of spiritual beings who do not have to enter earthly incarnation, but spend the aeons, during which we live, in an ethereal or other higher form of higher existence,—all these human, super-human and sub-human beings, belonged at that time to the all-embracing School of the Michael Power. They were, so to speak, disciples of Michael. And you will remember, last Monday I told you a little of the content of the teaching given at that time.

To-day we will begin by emphasising this one point: the previous Michael dominion, having lasted three centuries and finding its culmination in the Alexandrian epoch of pre-Christian time, was withdrawn from the earth, and the dominions of the other Archangeloi followed. At the time when on earth, within the earthly realm, the Mystery of Golgotha took place, the Michael community were united in the Spirit, with all the spiritual and human-spiritual beings who belonged to them. How did they feel and perceive the Mystery of Golgotha? Christ at that time was taking His departure from their realm—the realm of the Sun. Such was their experience; while the human beings who were then living upon earth had to experience the Mystery of Golgotha quite differently. For Christ was coming down to them to the earth.

Now this is an immense, far-reaching and gigantic contrast in experience, as between the one kind of human soul and the other,—a contrast which we need to penetrate and understand with all our heart and mind.

Then there began the time when the Cosmic Intelligence, that is to say, the essence of Intelligence that is spread out over the great universe, which had been subject to the unlimited rulership of Michael until the end of the Alexandrian epoch, gradually passed into the possession of man on earth and fell, so to speak, out of the hands of Michael.

You must realise, my dear friends: the evolution of mankind with respect to these things took place as follows. Till the end of the Alexandrian time, nay even afterwards,—and for certain groups of human beings long, long afterwards,—when a man was intelligent there was always the consciousness, not that he had evolved the Intelligence within him, but that he was gifted with it from the spiritual worlds. If a man thought a clever thought, the cleverness of it was ascribed to the inspiration of spiritual Beings. It is indeed of fairly recent date that man ascribes his cleverness, his intelligence, to himself. This is due to the fact that the rulership of Intelligence has passed from the hands of Michael into the hands of men. When Michael at the end of the eighteen-seventies again assumed his regency in the guidance of earthly destinies, he found the Cosmic Intelligence, which had fallen away from him entirely since the 8th or 9th century A.D.,—he found it again in the realm of mankind below.

Thus it was in the last third of the 19th century, when the Gabriel dominion was over and the Michael dominion began to spread. It was as though Michael, coming to the intelligent human beings, arrived at a point where he could say: Here do I find again that which has fallen away from me, which I administered in times long past.

Now in the Middle Ages there was a great conflict between the leading men of the Dominican Order and those who, in a continuation of Asiatic Alexandrianism, had found their way over into Spain,—Averroes, for example. What was the substance of this conflict? Averroes and those on his side—the Mohammedan followers of Aristotelian learning—said: " Intelligence is universal, common to all." They only spoke of a pan-Intelligence, not of an individual human Intelligence. To Averroes the individual human Intelligence was but a kind of mirrored reflection in the single human head. In its reality it had only a general, universal existence.

I will draw a mirror, thus (drawing on the blackboard). I might equally well have drawn a mirror not with nine parts only, but with hundreds, thousands and millions. Over against it is an object which will be reflected. So it was for Averroes, who was attacked so vigorously by Thomas Aquinas. For Averroes—in the tradition of the old Michael epoch—Intelligence was pan-Intelligence, one Intelligence and one only, which the several human heads reflected. As soon as the human head ceases to work, the individual Intelligence is no more. Now was this really true?

The fact is this. That which Averroes conceived had been true till the end of the Alexandrian age. It was simply a cosmic and human fact until the end of that age. But Averroes held fast to it while the Dominicans received into themselves the evolution of mankind. They said, " It is not so." They might of course have said, " It was so once, but it is not so to-day." But they did not say this. They simply took the actual and true condition at that time (the 13th century) which became even more so in the 14th and 15th centuries. They said: " Now everyone has his own intellect, his own intelligence."

This was what really happened, and to bring these matters

to full clearness of understanding was the very task of the supersensible School of which I spoke last Monday. It was repeated in that School again and again in many metamorphoses, inasmuch as the character of the ancient Mysteries was again and again described. Wonderfully clearly and visibly, not in supersensible Imaginations, (these only came at the beginning of the 19th century) but in supersensible Inspirations, there was described what I have often been able to give here in a reflected radiance—the essence of the ancient Mysteries.

Then too they pointed to the future, to what was to become the new life of the Mysteries. They pointed to all that was to come, though not in the way of the old Mysteries which had come to human beings who did not yet possess Intelligence on earth, and who, accordingly, still had a dream-like experience of supersensible worlds. They pointed to that new life of the Mysteries which we must now begin to understand in the realm of Anthroposophy, and which is absolutely compatible with the full Intelligence of man—the clear, light-filled Intelligence.

Let us now enter a little into the more intimate details of the teachings of that supersensible School. For they led to a knowledge of something, of which only a kind of shadowy reflection has existed in the world-conceptions of men upon the earth since the old Hebrew time and in the Christian era. It exists, to this day (when a far deeper insight ought already to prevail) in the large majority of men only as a dim reflection out of old traditions. I mean the teaching about Sin, about the sinful human being, the teaching about man, who at the beginning of human evolution was predestined not to descend so deeply into the material realm as he has actually descended.

We can still find a good version of this teaching in St. Martin, the 'Unknown Philosopher.' He still did teach his pupils that originally, before human evolution on the earth began, man stood upon a certain height from which he then sank down through a primeval Sin which St. Martin describes as the Cosmic Adultery. By a primeval Sin man descended to that estate in which he finds himself to-day.

St. Martin here points to something that was inherently contained in the doctrine of Sin during the whole of human evolution, I mean, the idea that man does not stand at that high level at which he *could* be standing. All teachings about inherited Sin were justly connected with this idea, that man has descended from the height which originally was his.

Now by following this idea to its conclusion, a world-conception of a very definite shade or colouring had gradually been evolved. This kind of world-conception said in effect: Man has become sinful (and to become sinful means to fall from one's original height). And since man has in fact become sinful, he cannot see the world as he would have been able to see it in his sinless condition before the Fall. Man, therefore, sees the world darkly and dimly. He sees it not in its true form. He sees it with many illusions and false fantasies. Above all, he sees what he sees in outer Nature, not as it really is or with its true spiritual background. He sees it in a material form which is not there in reality at all. Such was the meaning of the saying: Man is sinful. Such was its meaning in ancient time and—in the traditions—frequently even to this day. Thus upon earth too, those who had kept the tradition of the Mysteries continued to teach: Man cannot perceive the world, he cannot feel in the world, he cannot act in the world as he would think and feel and act if he had not become sinful,—if he had not descended from the height for which his Gods originally predestined him.

Now we may turn our gaze to all the leading Spirits in the kingdom of Archangeloi who follow one another in earthly rule, so that this earthly dominion is exercised by the several Archangeloi in turn through successive periods of three to three-and-a-half centuries. In the last three or four centuries it has been the dominion of Gabriel. Now it will be that of Michael, for three hundred years to come. Let us turn our gaze therefore to the whole series of these Archangel Beings: Gabriel, Raphael, Zachariel, Anael,

Oriphiel, Samael, Michael. As we look to all these Beings, we can characterise the relation that exists between them and the loftier Spirits of the Hierarchies, somewhat as follows.

I beg you not to take these words lightly or easily. We have but human words to express these sublime realities. Simple as the words may sound, they are not lightly meant. Of all these Angels, the number of whom is seven, six have to a very considerable extent (not entirely—Gabriel most of all—but even he not altogether)—six, as I said, have to a very considerable extent resigned themselves to the fact that man is faced with Maya, with the great illusion, because, in his quality which no longer accords with his original pre-destination, he has in fact descended from his first stature. Michael alone, Michael is the only one (I say again, I am forced to use banal expressions) Michael is the only one who would not give in. Michael, and with him those who are the Michael spirits even among men, continues to take this stand: I am the Ruler of the Intelligence. And the Intelligence must be so ruled that there shall not enter into it any illusion nor false fantasy, nor anything that would restrict the human being to a dark and vague and cloudy vision of the world.

My dear friends: to see how Michael stands there as the greatest opponent in the ranks of the Archangels, is an unspeakably uplifting sight,—overpowering, magnificent. And every time a Michael Age returned, it happened upon earth too that Intelligence as a means to knowledge became not only cosmopolitan as I have already said, but became such that men were filled through and through with the consciousness: We *can* after all ascend to the Divinity.

This consciousness: "We can after all ascend to the Divine," played an immense part at the end of the last Michael Age, the Michael Age before our own. Starting from ancient Greece, the places of the ancient Mysteries everywhere were in a state of discouragement; an atmosphere of discouragement had come over them all. Discouraged were those who lived on in Southern Italy and Sicily. The successors of the ancient Pythagorean School of the sixth pre-Christian century had been well-nigh extinguished. They were filled with discouragement.

Once again, those who were initiated in the Pythagorean Mysteries saw how much illusion, illusion of materialism, was spreading over the whole world.

Discouraged too were those who were the daughters and sons of ancient Egyptian Mysteries. Oh, these Egyptian Mysteries! It was only like the slag from wonderful old veins of precious metal, when they still handed down the deep old teachings, such as were expressed in the legend of Osiris, or in the worship of Serapis. And yonder in Asia where were those mighty and courageous ascents to the spiritual world that had taken their start, for example, from the Mysteries of Diana at Ephesus? Even the Samothracian Mysteries, the wisdom of the Kabiri, could now only be deciphered by individuals who bore deep within them the impulse of greatness to soar upward with might and main. By such souls alone could the clouds of smoke that ascended from Axieros, etc., from the Kabiri, be deciphered.

Discouragement everywhere! Everywhere a feeling of what they sought to overcome in the ancient Mysteries as they turned to the secret of the Sun Mystery, which is in truth the secret of Michael. Everywhere a feeling: Man cannot, he is unable.

This Michael Age was an age of great trial and probation. Plato, after all, was but a kind of watery extract of the ancient Mysteries. The most intellectual element of this extract was then extracted again in Aristotelianism, and Alexander took it on his shoulders.

This was the word of Michael at that time: Man must reach the Pan-Intelligence, he must take hold of the Divine upon earth in sinless form. From the centre of Alexandria the best that has been achieved must be spread far and wide in all directions, through all the places of the Mysteries, discouraged as they are. This was the impulse of Michael. This is indeed the relation of Michael to the other

Archangeloi. He has protested most strongly against the Fall of man.

This too was the most important content of his teaching, the teaching with which he instructed his own in the supersensible School of which I spoke last Monday. It was as follows: Now that the Intelligence will be down among men upon the earth, having fallen from the lap of Michael and from his hosts,—now in this new Age of Michael, men will have to become aware of the way of their salvation. They must not allow their Intelligence to be overcome by sinfulness; rather must they use this age of Intelligence to ascend to the spiritual life in purity of Intelligence, free from all illusion.

Such is the mood and feeling on the side of Michael as against the side of Ahriman. On Monday last I characterised this great contrast. Already the very strongest efforts are being made by Ahriman, and more still will be made in the future—the strongest efforts to acquire the Intelligence that has come into the hands of men. For if men once became possessed by Ahriman, Ahriman himself, in human heads, would be possessing the Intelligence.

My dear friends, we must learn to know this Ahriman, these hosts of Ahriman. It is not enough to find the name of Ahriman contemptible or to give the name of Ahriman to so many beings whom one despises. That is of no avail. The point is that in Ahriman there stands before us a cosmic Being of the highest imaginable Intelligence, a cosmic Being who has already taken the Intelligence entirely into the individual, personal element. In every conceivable direction Ahriman is in the highest degree intelligent, over-intelligent. He has at his command a dazzling Intelligence, proceeding from the whole human being, with the single exception of the part of the human being which in the human forehead takes on a human form.

To reproduce Ahriman in human Imaginations we should have to give him a receding forehead, a frivolously cynical expression, for in him everything comes out of the lower forces, and yet from these lower forces the highest Intelligence proceeds. If ever we let ourselves in for a discussion with Ahriman, we should inevitably be shattered by the logical conclusiveness, the magnificent certainty of aim with which he manipulates his arguments. The really decisive question for the world of men, in the opinion of Ahriman, is this: Will cleverness or stupidity prevail? And Ahriman calls stupidity everything that does not contain Intelligence within it in full personal individuality. Every Ahriman-being is over-endowed with personal Intelligence in the way I have now described; critical to a degree in the repudiation of all things unlogical; scornful and contemptuous in thought.

When we have Ahriman before us in this way, then too we shall feel the great contrast between Ahriman and Michael. For Michael is not in the least concerned with the personal quality of Intelligence. It is only for man that the temptation is ever-present to make his Intelligence personal after the pattern of Ahriman. Truth to tell, Ahriman has a most contemptuous judgment of Michael. He thinks Michael foolish and stupid,—stupid, needless to say, in relation to himself. For Michael does not wish to seize the Intelligence and make it personally his own. Michael only wills, and *has* willed through the thousands of years, nay through the aeons, to administer the Pan-Intelligence. And now once more, now that men have the Intelligence, it should again be administered by Michael as something belonging to all mankind—as the common and universal Intelligence that benefits all men alike.

We human beings shall indeed do rightly, my dear friends, if we say to ourselves: the idea that we can have cleverness for ourselves alone is foolish. Certainly we cannot be clever for ourselves alone. For if we want to prove anything to another person logically, the first thing we must presume is that the same logic holds good for him as for ourselves. And for a third party again it is the same logic. If anyone were able to have a logic of his own it would be absurd for us to want to prove anything to him by *our* logic. This after all is easy to realise; but it is essential in the present age of Michael for this realisation also to enter into our deepest feelings.

Thus behind the scenes of existence is raging the battle of Michael against all that is of Ahriman. And this, as I said last Monday, is among the tasks of the anthroposophist . . . He must have a feeling for the fact that these things are so at the present time. He must feel that the cosmos is as it were in the very midst of the battle.

You see, this battle was already there in the cosmos, but it became significant above all since the 8th or 9th century, when the Cosmic Intelligence gradually fell away from Michael and his hosts and came down to men on earth. It only became acute when the Spiritual Soul began to unfold in humanity, at the point of time which I have so often indicated, at the beginning of the 15th century. In individual spirits who lived on earth at that time, we see, even upon earth, some sort of reflection of what was taking place in the great supersensible School of which I spoke last Monday. We see something of it reflected in individual men on the earth.

In recent lectures we have said much of heavenly reflections in earthly schools and institutions. We have spoken of the great School of Chartres, and others. But we can speak of this in relation to individual human beings too. Thus at the very time when the Spiritual Soul began to evolve in civilised mankind—when Rosicrucianism, genuine Rosicrucianism, was nurturing the early beginnings of the impulse to the Spiritual Soul,—something of the impulse which was at work above the earth struck down like lightning upon a spirit living in that age. I mean Raymond of Sabunda. What he taught at the beginning of the 15th century is almost like an earthly reflection of the great supersensible doctrine of Michael which I have characterised.

He said: men have fallen from the vantage-point that was given to them originally by their Gods. If they had remained upon that point, they would have seen around them all that lives in the wondrous crystal shapes of the mineral kingdom, in the amorphous mineral kingdom, in the hundred-and-thousand fold forms of the plant kingdom, in the forms of the animal, all that lives and moves in water and air, in warmth and in the earthly realm. All this they would have seen as it really is, in its true nature.

Raymond of Sabunda called to mind, how the Tree of Sephiroth, or the Aristotelian categories (those generalised concepts that look so strange to one who cannot understand them) contain what is meant to guide us through Intelligence, up into the universe. How dry, how appallingly dry do these categories seem as they are taught in the text-books of Logic. Being, having, becoming, here, there—ten of these categories, ten abstract concepts, and people say: it is too dreadful, it is appalling to have to learn such abstractions. Why should anyone grow warm with enthusiasm for ten generalised concepts—being, having, becoming and so forth?

But it is just as though someone were to say: here is Goethe's *Faust*. Why do people make so much fuss of it? It only consists of A, B, C, D, E, F, . . . to Z. Nothing else is there in the book, only A, B, C, D . . . Z in various combinations and permutations. Certainly one who cannot read, and takes Goethe's *Faust* in hand, will not perceive the greatness that is contained in it. He will only see A, B, C, D . . . to Z. One who does not know how the A, B, C, D, are to be combined, who does not know how they are related to one another, cannot read Goethe's *Faust*.

So it is, in relation to the reading of words, with the Aristotelian categories. There are ten of them, not so many as the letters of the alphabet, but they are indeed the spiritual letters. And anyone who knows how to manipulate ' being,' ' having,' ' becoming,' etc., in the right way,—just as we must know how to treat the several letters so that they produce the *Faust* of Goethe,—anyone who knows how to do this, may still be able to divine what Aristotle for example said of these things in his instruction of Alexander.

Raymond of Sabunda was one who still drew attention to such things. He had knowledge of them. He said: Look for instance at what is still contained in Aristotelianism.

There we find something that has still remained of that old standpoint from which man fell at the beginning of human evolution on earth. Originally, men still preserved some memory of it. It was the reading in the Book of Nature. But men have fallen; they can no longer truly read in the Book of Nature. Hence God in His Compassion has given them in the Bible, the Book of Revelation, in order that they may not entirely depart from the Divine and Spiritual. Thus Raymond of Sabunda still taught, even in the 15th century, that the Book of Revelation exists for sinful man because he is no longer able to read in the Book of Nature. And in the way he taught these things, we can already perceive his idea that man must find once more the power to read in the great Book of Nature.

This is the impulse of Michael. Now that the Intelligence administered by him has come down to men, it is his impulse to lead men again to the point where they will read once more in the Book of Nature. The great Book of Nature will be opened again. Men will read once more in the Book of Nature.

In reality, everyone who is in the Anthroposophical Movement should feel that he can only understand his karma when he knows that he personally is called to read once more, spiritually, in the Book of Nature—to find the spiritual background of Nature, God having given His Revelation for the intervening time.

Read the inner meaning that is contained in my book *Mysticism at the Dawn of the Modern Spiritual Life* (*Modern Mysticism*).* On the last page you will see (in the form, of course, in which I could and had to write it at that time), you will see that the whole point was to guide the Anthroposophical Movement in this direction—to awaken once more the faculty to read not only in the Book of Revelation, in which I said that Jacob Boehme was still reading, but in the Book of Nature. The blundering, inadequate, and frequently repulsive attempts of modern natural science must be transmuted by a spiritual world-conception, till

* *Mysticism and Modern Thought.* Anthroposophical Publishing Co.

there arise from them a true reading of the Book of Nature. I think even this expression, ' the Book of Nature,' is to be found at the end of my book *Mysticism at the Dawn of the Modern Spiritual Life.* From the very beginning, the Anthroposophical Movement had this ' Shibboleth.' From the very beginning it was an appeal to those who should now listen to the voice of their own karma, and hear more or less dimly and subconsciously the call: ' Behold, my karma is somehow moved and taken hold of by this Michael message which is sounding forth into the world. I, through my own karma, have to do with this.'

There are the human beings after all, who have been always there. They are always there. They have come, and they will come ever and again. There are those who are prepared in some sense to depart from the world and come together in this which is now called the Anthroposophical Society. As to the sense in which this ' departure from the world ' is to be conceived—whether it be more or less real, or outwardly formal or the like—that is another matter. For the individual souls it *is* a kind of departure—a going away from the world and into something different from the world in which they have grown up. All manner of karmic experiences come to the individual, each in his own way. The one will have this or that to undergo through the fact that he must tear himself loose from old connections and unite with those who are seeking to cultivate the message of Michael. There are some who feel this union with the mission of Michael as a kind of salvation. There are others who feel it in a different way, finding themselves in this position: ' I am drawn to Michael on the one hand and to Ahrimanism on the other. I cannot choose. Through my life I stand in the midst of these things.' There are some whose inner courage tears them away, albeit they still preserve the outward connections. There are some who still find the outer connections easily. And this perhaps is best for the present condition of the Anthroposophical Society. But in every case, those human beings who are within the Anthroposophical Movement stand face to face with others who are not in it, including some with whom they are deeply, karmically connected from former earthly lives. Here we can look into the strangest of karmic threads.

My dear friends, we shall only be able to understand these karmic threads if we remember all the preceding conditions that we have now set forth. We shall only understand them when we have really seen how the souls who to-day, out of their unconscious Being, feel impelled to the Anthroposophical Movement, have undergone experiences together. For they have undergone much together in former lives on earth. Moreover the great majority of them belonged to the hosts who heard the Michael message in the supersensible in the 15th, 16th and 17th centuries, and who took part at the beginning of the 19th century in the great Imaginative ceremony of which I have here spoken. Thus we behold a mighty Cosmic and Tellurian call, addressed to the deep karmic relationship of the members of the Anthroposophical Society. We heard last Monday, how this call will continue throughout the 20th century, and how the culmination will come at the end of this century. Of these things, my dear friends, I will speak again next Sunday.

IX

Entry of the Michael Forces

Decisive Character of the Michael Impulses

You will have seen from the previous lectures, how the souls who out of the depths of their subconscious life feel impelled towards the Anthroposophical Movement, bear this impulse within them through their special relationship to the forces of Michael. We have accordingly considered the working of these Michael-forces throughout the centuries, in order to see what influence the impulses of Michael can have upon the lives of those who stand in any kind of connection with them.

Now the Michael impulses—and this is of great importance for the karma of every single anthroposophist—the Michael impulses are of a kind to enter deeply and intensely into the whole being of man. We know from previous descriptions that the rulership of Michael, if so we may call it, beginning for earthly life at the end of the eighteen-seventies, was preceded by the rulership of Gabriel; and I have described how the rulership of Gabriel is connected with forces that go through the line of physical inheritance—forces related to physical reproduction.

The forces of Michael are the very opposite of this. The rulership of Gabriel is characterised by the fact that his impulses enter strongly into the physical bodily nature of man. Michael, on the other hand, works intensely into the spiritual being of man. You can tell this from the very fact that he is the administrator of the Cosmic Intelligence. But Michael's impulses are strong and powerful. Taking their start from the spiritual, they work through and through the human being. They work into the spiritual, thence into the soul-nature, and thence again into the bodily nature of man. Now in the karmic connections of life, these super-earthly forces are constantly at work. Beings of the higher Hierarchies are working with man and upon him. It is thus that the karma of a man takes shape. And so it is with the Michael-forces. Working as they do upon the whole human being, they work also very strongly into his karma. Gabriel-forces work only very little—I do not say not at all—but very little into the essential karma of a human being. Michael-forces on the other hand work very strongly into his karma.

If, therefore, certain human beings—and this in the last resort applies to you all, my dear friends—if certain human beings are especially connected with the stream of Michael, their individual karmas can only be understood when thought of in connection with the stream of Michael.

Now Michael is a Spirit who stands in a special relationship to the Sun and to all Sun-impulses. This being the case, we shall realise what a profound significance his impulses must have for those who are especially exposed to them. In effect, his forces will work right into the physical organisation. For Michael-men therefore (if we may use this term), we must connect the physical phenomena of health and illness with karma in an even higher degree than for Gabriel- or Raphael-men, or the like. Things in the universe are very complicated; and although Raphael is the Spirit most intimately connected with the art of Healing, nevertheless it is Michael who brings the karma of men nearest of all to health and to disease.

There is another fact in this connection. The Michael-forces not only work in a cosmopolitan sense, but they also work in such a way as to tear a man out of the narrower earthly connections of his life and carry him up on to a spiritual height, where he feels the earthly connections less strongly than others do. At any rate his karma predestines him for this. This again has a profound influence upon the karma of every single man who belongs to the stream of Michael.

You see, in the last third of the 19th century it did really happen that human beings—I will not say of nervous temperament—but human beings intense in soul and spirit, were able to feel the penetration of the Michael-forces into the world. In those who were essentially men of Michael, this penetration of the Michael-forces into the world came to expression in this way: they felt many things, which other men would have passed by more or less indifferently, entering deeply and incisively into their lives.

Above all their karma was such that they had a strong feeling—though they did not understand it clearly—a strong feeling of the battle I described the day before yesterday, the battle between Michael and Ahriman. In the present age, Ahriman can only have a strong influence upon men when their consciousness is diverted in one way or another. The most radical phenomenon is that of a fainting fit, or a diminution of consciousness lasting for a considerable time. In times like this, when a man is overcome by faintness or diminution of consciousness, the Ahriman forces can most effectively approach him. At such times they work their way into him, he is exposed to them. But it was above all in the last third of the 19th century—and especially in the time when the end of the Kali Yuga was approaching, in the very last years of the 19th century,—it was a shattering experience to see behind the scenes of this external, physical world which is spread out before man's senses.

For directly adjoining this outer world there is a world revealing very, very much of those historic processes in which the higher supersensible Beings enter and play a part.

In the last third of the 19th century, and especially in the last decade, only a thin veil concealed that which we recognise as the dominion of Michael, the great battle of Michael and all the facts connected with him. Since then, Michael himself has been taking part in the battle even in the outer world, and we need a far stronger power to behold what is present supersensibly than was needed before the end of the Kali Yuga, when, as I said, the next adjoining world, where Michael was battling as yet behind the scenes, was severed from our own by a thin veil only.

But Michael insists, as I have told you, that his dominion shall prevail and penetrate at any cost. Michael is a Spirit filled with strength, and he can only make use of thoroughly brave men, men full of inner courage.

Now in the whole nexus that I have described, in the supersensible School of the 15th, 16th and 17th centuries, and in the great supersensible Cult of the beginning of the 19th century, among all the spirits who partake in these things, great numbers of Luciferic figures are all the time playing their part. The Luciferic figures are necessary, necessary in the whole connection of these things. Michael needs the Luciferic spirits, he needs their co-operation to overcome the polar antithesis of Ahriman. Thus the men of Michael are placed into the very midst of the battle—or, if we may not call it so—the surging waves of interplay, of Luciferic impulses and Ahrimanic.

Just at the end of the 19th century these things showed themselves with great clarity and definition. In those years it was by no means rarely that one caught a glimpse, through the veil, as I have called it. Then one saw how intensely Michael was having to battle against Ahriman, and how easy it was for the consciousness of men to be diverted by all manner of Luciferic influences.

You may say: Disturbances of consciousness, attacks of faintness and the like, are nothing out of the ordinary. Outwardly considered they are not, of course; but they can become most significant through that which happens as a consequence,—through that which ensues when the diversion or diminution of consciousness takes place. I will give you an example.

It was once a question of someone being made more intimately acquainted with a certain historic personality. He was to study an historic personality who had lived in the time of the Renaissance and Reformation. I want you to understand me precisely. All the preparations had been made for this man (it was at the end of the eighteen-nineties) to become historically acquainted with a personality who had lived at the time of the Renaissance and Reformation.

Indeed, with all the conditions that had gone before, it seemed scarcely possible for anything else to happen, than that he would become familiar with that historic personality in the perfectly ordinary, and if I may call it so, pedantic way of scholarship. But look what happened. Through the refined workings of karma he became incapable of using his consciousness just at the very time when he was to have had this experience. He fell into a kind of sleep from which he could not awaken, and was thus prevented.

Of course in ordinary life one pays little heed to such a thing. Yet it is through happenings like these that we look directly from the earthly into the spiritual world. And if you want an explanation of this fact, then we must say: This man, who was to have become historically acquainted with a certain personality of the time of the Renaissance and Reformation, would undoubtedly have received a very strong impression if he had had this experience. He did not have it; he missed it, he was prevented. But in that very time, the impression which he would have received was transformed. He received it in another form; it was transformed into a peculiar impressionability for the Michael element. He actually received, though unconsciously, a real power of understanding for the Michael element.

I give this somewhat strange example in order to show you by what paths the Michael element was approaching human beings at that time. We could give many examples of this kind. Indeed, human beings to-day would be quite different if such things had not occurred to many individuals. Such things may happen in hundreds of different ways. In the case I have just related, my dear friends, the man actually fell into a kind of sleep. In other cases it happened thus:—Some event that would have led a man away from Michael was prevented by a friend or someone else coming and taking him away to a different place, and his consciousness was veiled around in a most natural and matter-of-fact way. He was prevented from partaking in what was karmically set before him to begin with. It was just in those years that the strongest interferences took place with the ordinary smooth course of karma.

And as a rule in such cases it became evident how deeply these Michael influences work. In many instances one saw that such human beings had been affected not only in soul but even down into the body when their karma had received a jerk of this kind, because Michael needed to enter through the portals of a human consciousness into the earthly world of sense.

It is interesting in the highest degree to see how in the eighteen-nineties men were led into events which were none other than the paths of Michael from the spiritual into the physical world. For you must remember, the entry of Michael into the physical world was taking place in the last third of the 19th century. But it had been prepared for, in the spiritual world, for a long time before—already since the beginning of the eighteen-forties. If I may put it so, Michael and his hosts were drawing ever nearer and nearer, and it became more and more evident that those human beings would now descend, who in their earthly destiny were connected with the task of Michael,—the task of receiving the Intelligence here upon earth again after it had fallen away from the hosts of Michael in the supersensible world.

Into the midst of all these things, as you will recognise from my presentation of the Mysteries, the Anthroposophical Movement is placed. For the Anthroposophical Movement is connected, as you will see from former lectures, with this whole stream of Michael.

Now I want you to consider in this light the karmic conditions of individual human beings who are led by an inner urge to approach the Anthroposophical Movement. They come, to begin with, from the world. They stand in many connections in the world. There have indeed been many communities in the world's history in which human beings have become united. But there was never a cohesive power of that peculiar quality which the Michael forces engender. Hence a peculiar situation is brought about for those who find their way, from other connections in the world, into the Anthroposophical Society. One can find one's way into other societies too, and could always do so, but one's destiny did not need to be very deeply affected. Into the Anthroposophical Society one cannot come—not at least in a thoroughly sincere way that really moves the soul—without being deeply and fundamentally influenced in one's destiny. This becomes especially clear when we consider these things along a right line of approach.

Take a human being who is just coming into the Anthroposophical Society, and who until then had certain connections with non-anthroposophists, which he may perhaps still continue to have. The difference between the one who stands within and the one who stands or remains outside, is of far greater significance than in the case of any other communities. There are two kinds of relationships.

Through the fulfilment of all the things I have described, we are living, once and for all, in a time of great, immense decisions. Thus the standing side-by-side to-day of anthroposophists and non-anthroposophists is fraught with great decisions. Either it is a question of the dissolving of old karma for the one who is in the Anthroposophical Society, or it is a question of the weaving of new karma for the one who is outside it. And these are great differences.

Let us assume an anthroposophist stands very near in life to a non-anthroposophist. It may be to begin with that the anthroposophist has old karmic connections to settle with the non-anthroposophist. On the other hand it may be that the non-anthroposophist has to enter into karmic connections with the anthroposophist, for the future. At any rate these are the only two cases I have hitherto been able to observe, though of course they are of many different kinds. There are no intermediates, there are no others beside these two. From this you will see that this is really a time of great decisions, for, if we may describe it so, either non-anthroposophists are being influenced in such a way that they come to the Michael community, or else the influences work in such a way that those who do not belong to the Michael community will be avoided by it. This indeed is the time of great decisions—the great crisis to which the sacred books of all time have referred—for in reality the present age is meant. Such indeed is the peculiar nature of the Michael impulses: they are fraught with great decisions, and they become decisive especially in this our age.

Human beings who in the present incarnation receive the Michael impulses through Anthroposophy, are thereby preparing their whole being in such a way that these Michael impulses enter even into the forces that are otherwise determined merely by the connections of race and nation.

Think how much this means:—Here is a man who stands within some national group. We can see at once, he is a Russian, he is a Frenchman, he is an Englishman, he is a German. We recognise it by his appearance, and we locate him by thinking, as we see him, where can this man belong? We think it a matter of some importance if we can recognise: he is a Turk, he is a Russian, or the like. Now with those who to-day receive Anthroposophy with inner force of soul, with deep impulse and strength of heart—who receive it, therefore, as the deepest force of their life—such distinctions will have no more meaning when next they return to earth. People will say: Where does he come from? He is not of any nation, he is not of any race, he is as though he had grown away from all races and nations.

When the last Michael dominion took place, in the age of Alexander, the point was to spread Grecian culture in a cosmopolitan way, carrying it out in all directions. The campaigns of Alexander were an immense achievement in the equalising of men on earth, I mean in the spreading among them of a common element. But the thing was not yet able to strike so deep, for at that time Michael still administered the *Cosmic* Intelligence. Now Intelligence is on the earth, now it strikes far deeper, it strikes down even into the earthly element of man. For the first time, the Spiritual is preparing to become a race-creating force. The time will come when one will no longer be able to say: the man looks as if he belonged to this or that country,—he is a Turk, or an Arabian, an Englishman, a Russian or a German,—but one will have to say what will amount to this: 'In a former life on earth this man felt impelled to turn towards the Spirit in the sense of Michael.' Thus, that which is influenced by Michael will appear as an immediate, physically creative, physically formative power.

Now this is a thing that takes root deeply, very deeply in the karma of the individual. Hence the strange destiny of those who are sincere anthroposophists, the strange destiny that they are not able to come to terms with the world; they cannot quite master it, and yet at the same time they have to approach the world and enter into it with full earnestness.

I have said that those who stand with full intensity within the Anthroposophical Movement will return at the end of the century, and others will then unite with them, for by this means the salvation of the earth and earthly civilisation from destruction must eventually be settled. This is the mission of the Anthroposophical Movement, which weighs on the one hand so heavily upon one's heart, while on the other hand it moves the heart, uplifts it with enthusiasm. This mission we must understand and see.

It is most necessary for the anthroposophist to know that in this situation as an anthroposophist his karma will be harder to experience than it is for other men. From the very outset those who come into the Anthroposophical Society are predestined to a harder, more difficult experience of karma than other men. And if we try to pass this harder experience by—if we want to experience our karma in a comfortable way—it will surely take vengeance on us in one direction or another. We must be anthroposophists in our experience of karma too. To be true anthroposophists we must be able to observe our own experience of karma with constant wide-awake attention. If we do not, then our comfortable, easy-going experiencing of our karma—or rather our desire to experience it so—will find expression and take vengeance in physical illnesses, physical accidents and the like.

These finer, more intimate connections of life must indeed be seen and observed, for then we shall see many another thing besides. It is the best preparation for true and real spiritual sight, to observe these more intimate connections of life attentively. It is a wrong principle to want to evolve all manner of nebulous, abnormal, visionary states. On the other hand it is immensely right to occupy oneself with all that goes on more finely and intimately in the connections of destiny which we can recognise.

Do we not see how this becomes our karma, my dear friends: we live, or have lived, alongside of human beings who are absolutely prevented, inwardly prevented, from coming near to things anthroposophical. They are prevented, in spite of all that we—I will not say have brought to them of Anthroposophy—but that we might have brought to them if they would only take it. We see this happen, surely. Now this also is among the great decisions of present-day life. For the things that take place in this way will have great karmic significance, both for the one who comes into the Anthroposophical Movement and for the one who remains outside it. It will have extraordinary significance.

Let us imagine that these human beings meet one another again in a future incarnation. We know that what happens to us in future incarnations is already being prepared for in this present. The meeting-again with human beings to whom we are related in the way I have just described, will be such that the usual strangeness between man and man will be essentially enhanced. For Michael works right down into the physical sympathies and antipathies. Now all this is taking place already now in a preparatory way, for every single anthroposophist. It is immensely important for an anthroposophist to study just those karmic relationships which unfold between him and non-anthroposophists. For in this connection things are taking place which reach up into the next kingdom of the Hierarchies. For you must see, there is a counterpart to what I have just described, when I said that the Michael impulses appear as a race-creating force. There is a counterpart to it.

Let us take the following karmic instance. Someone is taken hold of in the very highest degree by the impulses of Anthroposophy. He is taken hold of in heart and mind, in soul and spirit. In such a case something will necessarily happen, which, expressed in words, sounds very strange indeed; and yet it is necessary. In such a case the Angel of the man must learn something. This is a thing of untold significance. The destiny of anthroposophists,—the destiny that works itself out between anthroposophists and non-anthroposophists,—casts its waves even into the worlds of the Angeloi. It leads to a parting of the Spirits, even in the world of the Angeloi. The Angel who accompanies the anthroposophist to his next incarnations learns to find his way still more deeply into the spiritual kingdoms than he could do before, while the Angel who belongs to the other man—to the one who cannot enter,—descends. It is in the destiny of the Angeloi that we first perceive how this great separation is taking place. To this, my dear friends, I would now direct your hearts. It is happening now, that the comparatively single and uniform kingdom of the Angeloi is being turned into a twofold kingdom of Angeloi, a kingdom of Angeloi with an upward tendency into the higher worlds, and with a downward tendency into lower worlds.

While the Michael community is being formed here upon earth, we can behold above it the ascending and the descending Angeloi. Looking more deeply into the world to-day, one can perpetually observe these streams, which are such as to stir the heart to its foundations.

Now I have told you that those who come into the anthroposophical life fall into two main groups. There are the ones who still carry into it a knowledge from the old heathen times, and have had little experience of that Christian development which took its course during the Kali Yuga. They have gone on evolving out of the old Pagan sources, and they now grow into the Christianity which is to be a cosmic Christianity once more. They are souls with a Pagan predestination, who in reality are only now growing into Christianity. The others are souls who are a little weary of

Paganism, though they do not confess this to themselves. From the outset they grow into the Anthroposophical Movement on account of its Christian character, but they do not enter so deeply into the anthroposophical Cosmology, the anthroposophical Anthropology, and so forth. They enter, rather, into the more abstractly religious side. These two groups are clearly to be distinguished.

Now for the group of a more Pagan predestination it is particularly necessary to take hold of the sustaining forces of Anthroposophy with full intensity of inner life. For this group, it is most necessary to avoid all side-tracks and other considerations, and steer straight forward in the direction of the anthroposophical sustaining forces.

We can only grasp these things when we receive them in our hearts; but they *must* enter into the hearts of anthroposophists. For only then will a real living-together within the Anthroposophical Society be possible, on a true anthroposophical foundation. When the more Pagan kind of souls, if I may call them so, bring forth their forces, which are in many cases already there in this incarnation deep within their souls, though they will often only come forth with difficulty,—when as I say they do bring forth the forces that are there in them, then there will spread over the whole Anthroposophical Society an atmosphere of steady and courageous progress in the good sense of Michael.

If this is to be so, we must have the courage to look straight into the intense conflict that is taking place, as between the things that Michael must undertake to achieve his great task, and the things that Ahriman is perpetually placing in his way.

Ahriman has already taken hold of certain tendencies in civilisation and placed them in his service. Consider this one fact:—Only since the 15th century has it become most thoroughly possible for man to take hold of the Intelligence. For since that time the Spiritual Soul is present in man, and the Spiritual Soul is man's very own; therefore it can make the Intelligence its very own. Moreover it is only since that time that those things have come to men, which have made them so exceedingly keen—if I may say so—on their own personal Intelligence.

Make this little calculation; it embraces huge dimensions, though the greatness of it be only in a spatial sense. Try to make this little calculation, my dear friends. Add up in thought all that is being thought to-day within a single day by all the writers in newspapers over the whole earth, so that newspapers may be produced. Try to imagine the tremendous sum-total of Intelligence that is being chewed out from their pens, put on to paper, printed, and so on. See what an enormous amount of personal Intelligence is flooding through the world. And now go back a few centuries, go back into the 13th century, and see whether such a thing is there at all. It is *simply not there*, there can be no question of its being there.

But I will give you another task. Imagine in your thought (to-day is Sunday, it is a good opportunity) just imagine how many meetings are being held on political questions from West to East,—we need not go beyond Europe for the moment. Here again, how much personal Intelligence is flooding through the atmosphere of the earth! And now imagine yourself in the 13th century. They managed without the newspapers and without the meetings. None of these things existed. Compare the 13th century with the present time. We may put it thus:—When you transplant yourself into the 13th century you can look out over the world, your vision is clear and unobstructed. There are no editorial offices, no political meetings, none of these. You look through, clear and free. But to-day, as you look over the world, everywhere the waves of personal Intelligence are surging forth. They are there everywhere. You simply cannot penetrate. It is a spiritual air that you could cut with a knife, as in some meeting-rooms where everyone is smoking his pipe or his cigar like a chimney-pot, and you say 'it is an air that you could cut with a knife.' So is the spiritual atmosphere to-day.

Such differences must be considered, if we would judge at all truly of the succession of historic epochs. When you read historians like Ranke you see nothing of these things, yet these are the real facts of history.

And all this that has come about since the 13th century, what is it? It is spiritual nourishment for the Ahrimanic Powers. Here in this region, they are first able to make their attacks. Hence the possibilities for Ahriman to take a hand in civilisation have become ever greater and greater. Needless to say, Spirits like Ahriman are not there to incarnate in physical bodies on the earth. Nevertheless, they *can* work on the earth, not indeed by incarnating but by incorporating themselves for certain spaces of time; when in one man or another there happens what I mentioned before: a diminution or diversion of consciousness. At such moments the human being provides a vehicle, and Ahriman is able,—not indeed to incarnate,—but to incorporate himself and to work out of that human being, with that human being's faculties.

It will be my further task to tell you of this kind of working of the Ahrimanic Powers. I shall have to show, for example, how Ahriman has appeared in the course of modern time even as an author. This will show you what things must be observed to-day by those who would fain observe realities.

X

The Michaelites: Their Karmic Impulse towards the Spiritual Life.—The Working of Ahriman into the once Cosmic and now Personal Intelligence

The fundamental feeling which I have wanted to call forth is this:—The individual who finds himself within the Anthroposophical Movement should begin to feel something of the peculiar karmic position which the impulse to Anthroposophy gives to a man. We cannot but confess that in the ordinary course of life man feels very little of his karma. He confronts his life as though the things that become his life's experience happened by fortuitious concatenations of circumstance. He pays little heed to the fact that the things that meet him in earthly life from birth till death contain the inner, karmic relationships of destiny. Or, if he does not consider this, he is all too prone to believe that a kind of fatalism is herein expressed,—and that human freedom is thereby called into question, and the like.

I have often said that the more intensely we penetrate the karmic connections, the more do we see the true essence of freedom. We need not therefore fear that by entering into the karmic relationships more accurately we shall lose our open and unimpaired vision of the essence of human freedom. I have described the matters connected with the former earthly lives of those who come into the Michael community, and with their lives between death and a new birth. You will have seen that with all such human beings—that is to say, in the last resort, with all of you—it is of the greatest importance, that the Spiritual plays a deep and significant part in the whole inner configuration of the soul.

In our materialistic age with all its conditions of life, of education and upbringing, a man can only come sincerely to a thing like Anthroposophy (otherwise his coming to it is insincere)—he can only come to it sincerely through the fact that he bears within him a karmic impulse impelling him towards the Spiritual. In this karmic impulse are summed up all those experiences which he underwent in the way I have described before he came down into the present earthly life.

Now, my dear friends, when a man is thus strongly united with spiritual impulses which work immediately upon his soul, he will as he descends from the spiritual into the physical worlds, enter less deeply, unite himself less strongly with the external, bodily nature. All those who have grown into the Michael stream as above described, were thus predestined to enter into this physical body with a certain reservation, if I may put it so. This too lies deep in the karma of the souls of anthroposophists.

In those, on the other hand, who out of an inner impulse quite consciously and anxiously hold themselves at a distance from things anthroposophical, we shall always find that they are fully and firmly established in the physical bodily nature. In the men of to-day who turn to that spiritual life which Anthroposophy would give, we find a looser relationship at any rate of the astral body and Ego-organisation with the physical and etheric organisation.

Now this means that such a man will less easily come to terms with his life. He will find life less easy to deal with, for the simple reason that he has more possibilities to choose from than other men. And he easily *grows out* of the very things that other men easily *grow into*. Think only, my dear friends, to what an intense degree many a human being of to-day *is* what the connections of outer life have made of him. No one can doubt that he fits into these connections, however questionable the thing may sometimes be in other respects. We see him as a clerk, a City man, a Builder, a Contractor, a Captain of industry and so forth. He is what he is as an absolute matter of course. There is no question about it. True, such a man will sometimes say he feels he was born for a better, or at any rate a different kind of life; but such a saying is not taken so very seriously. And now compare the infinite difficulties we find in those who are drawn by an inner impulse into the spiritual life of Anthroposophy. Perhaps we see it nowhere with such remarkable intensity as in the youth, and notably the youngest of the youth.

Take for instance the older pupils of the Waldorf School, those in the top classes of the school. We find, both in our boy and girl pupils, that they progress comparatively quickly in their development of soul and mind and spirit. But this does not make life any easier to take hold of for the young people. On the contrary, it generally becomes more difficult—being, as it is, more complicated. The possibilities become wider and more far-reaching. In the ordinary course of modern life, (certain exceptions being omitted) it is not overwhelmingly difficult for those who stand as teachers or educators beside the growing adolescent, to find the ways and means of giving sound advice. But when we bring our children on as we do in the Waldorf School, it becomes far more difficult to give advice, for the simple reason that the universal humanity is more developed in them. The wide horizon which the boy or girl acquires in the Waldorf School, places before their inner vision a greater number of possibilities.

Hence it is so necessary for Waldorf teachers—who again have been guided to this calling by their karma—to acquire a wide horizon and a broad outlook, a knowledge of the world and a sound feeling of what is going on in the world. At this point all the detailed educational principles and methods are far less important than wideness of outlook. Here again, in the karma of such a teacher, we see how large the number of possibilities becomes; far, far greater than in ordinary life. The child or adolescent confronts the Waldorf teacher, once again, not with definite and defined, but with manifold riddles,—differentiated in all conceivable directions.

The real karmic conditions and pre-disposing causes of

all that impels a man to Anthroposophy will best be understood if we speak not in pedantic outline and definition, but rather hint at the things in one way or another, characterising more the atmosphere in which, if I may put it so, anthroposophists unfold their lives.

All this makes it necessary for the anthroposophist to pay heed to *one* condition of his karma—a condition that is sure to be present in him to a high degree. Much can be said,—and we shall still have to say many things—about the reasons why one or another character or temperament is drawn to Anthroposophy after the events of the spiritual world which I have described. But all these impulses, which bring the single anthroposophists to Anthroposophy, have as it were one counterpart, which the Spirit of the World has made more strong in them than in other men. All the many possibilities that are there with respect to the most manifold things in life, demand from the anthroposophist initiative—inner initiative of soul. We must become aware of this. For the anthroposophist this proverb must hold good. He must say to himself: "Now that I have become an anthroposophist through my karma, the impulses which have been able to draw me to Anthroposophy require me to be attentive and alert. For somehow or somewhere, more or less deeply in my soul, there will emerge the necessity for me to find *inner initiative* in life,—initiative of soul which will enable me to undertake something or to make some judgment or decision out of my own inmost being." Verily, this is written in the karma of every single anthroposophist: "Be a man of initiative, and beware lest through hindrances of your own body, or hindrances that otherwise come in your way, you do not find the centre of your being, where is the source of your initiative. Observe that in your life all joy and sorrow, all happiness and pain will depend on the finding or not finding of your own individual initiative." This should stand written as though in golden letters, constantly before the soul of the anthroposophist. Initiative lies in his karma, and much of what meets him in this life will depend on the extent to which he can become willingly, actively conscious of it.

You must realise that very, very much has been said in these few words. For in our time there is extraordinarily much that can lead one astray with respect to all that guides and directs one's judgment; and without clear judgment on the conditions of life, initiative will not find its way forth from the deep foundations of the soul. Now what is it that can bring us to clear judgment on the things of life, especially in this our age? My dear friends, let us here consider one of the most important and characteristic features of our time. Let us then answer the question: How can we come to a certain clarity of judgment in face of it?

You will see presently that in what I am now going to tell you we have a kind of " egg of Colombus." With the egg of Columbus the point was to have the happy idea—how to set it up so that it would stand. In what I shall now tell you the point will also be to have the happy idea.

We live in the age of materialism. All that is taking place, by forces of destiny around us and within us, stands in the sign of materialism on the one hand, and of the intellectualism that is already so widespread, on the other. I characterised this intellectualism yesterday when I spoke of journalism and of the impulse everywhere to expatiate on the affairs of the world in public meetings, mass meetings and the like. We must become aware, to what an extent the man of to-day is subject to the influences of these two currents of the time. For it is almost as impossible to escape from these two, from intellectualism and materialism, as it is to avoid getting wet if you go out in the rain without an umbrella. These things are around us everywhere. After all, there are certain things we simply cannot know (and yet we have to know),—which we cannot know unless we read them in the papers. There are certain things we cannot learn (and we *have* to learn them) unless we learn them in the sense of materialism. How is one to become a doctor to-day, unless he is willing to consume a goodly portion of materialism? He can do no other than take the materialism too. He must do so as a matter of course, and if he is unwilling to do so he cannot become a proper doctor in the sense of the present age. Thus we are perpetually exposed to these things. This surely enters very strongly indeed into our karma.

Now all these things are as though created purposely to undermine initiative in the souls of men. Every public meeting, every mass meeting to which we go, only fulfils its purpose as such, if the initiative of the individual human being, with the exception of the speakers and leaders, is undermined. Nor does any newspaper fulfil its purpose if it does not create an atmosphere of opinion, thus undermining the individual's initiative.

These things must be seen. Moreover, we must remember that this ordinary consciousness of man is a very tiny chamber in the soul, while all that is going on around him, in the forms which I have just described, has a gigantic influence on his sub-conscious life. And after all, we have no alternative. Beside the fact that we are human beings pure and simple, we must be " contemporaries " of our age. Some people think it is possible in a given age to be a human being pure and simple, but this too would lead to our downfall. We must also be men and women of our age. Of course it is bad if we are no more than this; but we *must* be contemporaries of our age, that is to say, we must have a feeling of what is going on in our own time.

Now it is true that many anthroposophists let their minds be carried away from a living feeling of what is present in their time. For they prefer to paddle in the Timeless. In this respect one has the strangest experiences in conversation with anthroposophists. They are very well aware, for instance, who Lycurgus was, but their ignorance of their contemporaries, every now and then, is simply touching.

This too is due to the fact that such a man is pre-disposed to the unfolding of inner initiative. His karma having placed him in the world with this quality, he is always in the position (forgive the comparison) of a bee that has a sting but is afraid to use it at the right moment. The sting is the initiative, but the man is afraid to use it. He is afraid, above all, of stinging into the Ahrimanic realm. Not that he fears that he will thereby hurt the Ahrimanic. No, he is afraid that the sting will recoil into his own body. This, to some extent, is what his fear is like. Thus through an undetermined fear of life the initiative remains inactive.

These are the things which we must see through. On all hands, theoretically and practically, we meet with the materialism of our time. It is powerful, and we let our initiative be put off by it. If an anthroposophist has a sense for these things, he will perceive how he is being confused, put off, thrown back on every hand by materialism theoretical and practical, even in the deepest impulses of his will. Now this gives a peculiar form to his karma. If you will observe yourselves truly, you will discover it in your lives day by day, from morning until evening. And out of all this there naturally arises as a prevalent feeling of life: How shall I prove, theoretically and practically, the falsehood of materialism? This impulse lives in the hearts and minds of many anthroposophists. Somehow or other they want to convict materialism of falsehood. It is the riddle of life, the riddle that life has set so many of us in theory and practice: How shall we contrive to prove the falsehood of materialism?

Here is one who has been through the schools and has become a learned man. You will find many an example in the Anthroposophical Society. Now he is awakened to be an anthroposophist. He feels a tremendous impulse to refute materialism, to fight it, to say all manner of things against it. So he begins to attack and refute materialism, and maybe he thinks that in this very act he stands most thoroughly within the stream of Michael. But as a rule he meets with little success, and we cannot but admit: these things that are said against materialism, though they often proceed from a thoroughly good will, do not succeed. They make no impression upon the materialist in theory or practice. Why not?

This is the very thing that hinders our clarity of judgment. Here stands the anthroposophist. In order not to be hampered in his initiative, he wants to be clear what it is that confronts him in materialism. He wants to probe the wrongness of materialism to its foundations. But as a rule he finds little success. He thinks he is refuting materialism, but it is ever on its legs again. Why is this so?

Now comes what I have called the egg of Colombus. Why is it so, my dear friends? It is due to the simple fact that materialism is true. I have said this many times. Materialism is not wrong, it is quite right. Here lies the reason. And the anthroposophist should learn in a very special way the lesson that materialism is right. He should learn it in this way:—Materialism is right, but it holds good of the outer physical body *only*. The others, who are materialists, know the physical only,—or at least they think they know it. Here lies the error, not in the materialism itself. When we learn anatomy or physiology or practical outer life in the materialistic way we learn the truth, but it holds good in the physical alone. This confession must be made out of the inmost depths of our human being. I mean, the confession that materialism is right *in its own domain*—nay more, that it is the splendid achievement of our age to have discovered what is right and true in the domain of materialism. But the thing also has its practical, its karmically practical aspect.

This is what will happen in the karma of many an anthroposophist. He will come to have the feeling: Here am I living with human beings with whom indeed karma has united me. (I spoke of this yesterday). Here am I living with human beings who know materialism only. They only know what is true of the physical life, and they cannot approach Anthroposophy because they are put off by the very correctness of the knowledge that they have.

Now, my dear friends, we live in the age of Michael, and in our souls is the Intellectuality that fell from Michael. When Michael himself administered the Cosmic Intelligence, these things were different. From the materialism of that time, the Cosmic Intelligence was ever and again tearing his soul away. There were of course materialists even in former ages, but not as in our age. In former ages a man might be a materialist. Then with his Ego and astral body he was implanted in his physical and etheric body. He felt his physical body. But the Cosmic Intelligence, that Michael administered, tore his soul away from it ever and again. To-day we are side by side—indeed we are often karmically united—with men in whom it is as follows. They too have the physical body; but the Cosmic Intelligence has fallen away from Michael and is living individually,—personally, as it were,—in the human being. Hence the Ego—all that is soul and spirit—remains in the physical body. Thus there are standing, side by side with us, men whose soul and spirit has dived deep down into their physical body.

When we stand side by side with non-spiritual human beings, we must see these things according to the truth. Our standing beside them must not merely call forth in us sympathy or antipathy in the ordinary sense. It must be an experience that moves our soul deeply, and it can indeed be a shattering experience, my dear friends.

To realise how tragic, how deeply moving an experience it must be, to stand thus side by side with materialists (who, as I said before, are right in their own way) we need only look at those among them who are often highly gifted and who out of certain instincts may have very good impulses indeed; yet they cannot come to spirituality. We see the tragedy of it when we come to consider the great gifts and noble qualities of many of those who are materialists. For after all, there can be no question but that they who in this time of great decisions do not find their way to the Spirit, will suffer harm in their soul-life for the next incarnation. Great as their qualities may be, they will suffer harm. And when we see how through their karma a number of human beings to-day have the inner impulse to spirituality while others cannot come near to it,—when we behold this contrast—our karmic living-together with such as I have here described should find a deep response within our souls. It should touch us and move us with a sense of tragedy. Until it does so, we shall never come to terms with our own karma. For if we sum up all that I have said of Michaelism, (if I may now so call it) then we shall find: the Michaelites are indeed taken hold of in their souls by a power that is seeking to work from the Spiritual into the full human being, even down into the Physical. I described it yesterday as follows. I said: these human beings will put aside the element of race,—the element which, from natural foundations of existence, gives the human being such or such a stamp. If a man is taken hold of by the Spirit in this earthly incarnation inasmuch as he now becomes an anthroposophist he is thereby prepared in future to become a man no longer distinguished by such external features but distinguished rather by what he was in the present incarnation. Let us be conscious of this in all humility: The time will come when in these human beings the Spirit will reveal its own power to form the physiognomy,—to shape the whole form of man.

Such a thing has never yet been revealed in the history of the world. Hitherto the physiognomies of men have been formed on the basis of their nationality, out of the Physical. To-day we can still tell by the physiognomy of men, where they hail from,—especially when they are young, when the cares of life or the joys and divine enthusiasms of life have not yet left their mark. But in the time to come there will be human beings by whose physiognomy and features alone one will be able to tell what they were in their past incarnation. One will know that in their past incarnation they penetrated to the things of the Spirit. Then will the others stand beside them, and what will their karma then signify? It will have cast aside the ordinary karmic affinities.

My dear friends, in this respect he above all who knows how to take life in real earnest will tell you: One has been karmically united, or is still karmically united, with many who cannot find their way into this spirituality. And however many a kinship may still be left in life, one feels a more or less deep estrangement, a justified estrangement. The karmic connection, as it would work itself out in ordinary life, falls away; it goes. But it remains for something different. I would put it in this way:—From the one who stands outside in the field of materialism to the one who stands in the field of spirituality, nothing else will remain of karma; but this one thing will remain, that he must see him. He will become attentive to him. We can look to a time in the future, when those who in the course of the 20th century are coming ever more into the things of the Spirit, will stand side by side with others who were karmically united with them in the former life on earth. In that future time the karmic affinities, the karmic relationships, will make themselves felt far less. But of all the karmic relationships this will have remained: Those who are standing in the field of materialism will have to see and witness those who stand in the field of spirituality. Those who were materialists to-day will in the future have to look continually upon those who came to the things of the Spirit. This will have been left of karma.

Once again a shattering, a deeply moving act, my dear friends. And to what end? Truly it lies in a far-reaching Divine cosmic plan. For how will the materialists of to-day let anything be proved to them? By having it before their eyes—by being able to touch it with their hands. Those who stand in the field of materialism will be able to see with their eyes and touch with their hands those with whom they once were karmically united, perceiving in their physiognomy, in their whole expression, what the Spirit really is, for it will have become creative in outer form and feature. In such human beings it will thus be proved, visibly for the eyes of man, what the Spirit is as a creative power in the world. And it will be part of the karma of anthroposophists to demonstrate, for those who stand in the field of materialism to-day, that the Spirit truly *is*, and proves itself in man himself, through the wise councils of the Gods.

But to come to this, it is necessary for us to confront intellectualism, not in a vague and nebulous and ill-advised way, but truly. We must not go out, my dear friends, without an umbrella. I mean, we are exposed to all that I described above as the two streams—all the writing in the papers, all the talking in public meetings. As we cannot escape becoming wet if we go out without umbrellas, so these things too come over us, we cannot escape them. In the tenderest age of childhood,—when we are twenty to twenty-four years old—we have to pursue our studies (whatever they may be) through materialistic books. Yes, in this tender age of childhood—the age of twenty to twenty-four—they take good care to saturate and well prepare our inner life. For, as we study what is there put before us, we are trained in materialism by the very structure and configuration of the sentences. We are utterly defenceless. There is no help for it.

Such a thing cannot be countered by merely formal arguments. We cannot keep a man of to-day from being exposed to intellectual materialism. To write non-materialistic text-books on botany or anatomy to-day, simply would not do. The connections of life will not permit of it. The point is, my dear friends, that we should take hold of these things in no merely formal sense but in their reality. We must understand that since Michael no longer draws out the soul-and-spirit from the physical bodily nature as in times past, Ahriman can play his game with the soul-and-spirit as it lives within the body. Above all when the soul-spiritual is highly gifted and is yet firmly fastened in the body, then especially it can be exposed to Ahriman. Precisely in the most gifted of men does Ahriman find his prey,—so as to tear the Intelligence from Michael, remove it far from Michael. At this point something happens which plays a far greater part in our time than is generally thought. The Ahrimanic spirits, though they cannot incarnate, can incorporate themselves; temporarily they can penetrate human souls, permeate human bodies. In such moments the brilliant and overpowering spirit of an Ahrimanic Intelligence is stronger than anything that the individual being possesses,—far, far stronger. Then, however intelligent he may be, however much he may have learned, and especially if his physical body is thoroughly taken hold of by all his learning, an Ahrimanic spirit can for a time incorporate itself in him. Then it is Ahriman who looks out of his eyes, Ahriman who moves his fingers, Ahriman who blows his nose, Ahriman who walks.

Anthroposophists must not recoil from knowledge such as this. For such a thing alone can bring the realities of intellectualism before our souls. Ahriman is a great and outstanding Intelligence, and Ahriman's purpose with earthly evolution is overwhelming and thorough. He makes use of every opportunity. If the Spiritual has implanted itself so strongly in the bodily nature of a human being,—if the bodily nature is taken hold of by the Spirit to such an extent that the consciousness is thereby in a measure stunned or lowered or impaired,—Ahriman uses his opportunity. And then it happens (for in our age this has become possible) then it happens that a brilliant spirit takes possession of the human being, overpowering the human personality; and such a spirit, dwelling within a human personality and overpowering him, is able to work upon earth—able to work just like a human being.

This is the immediate striving of Ahriman, and it is strong. I have told you, my dear friends, of what will be fulfilled at the end of this century, with those who now come to the things of the Spirit and take them in full earnestness and sincerity. This is the time above all, which the Ahrimanic spirits wish to use most strongly. This is the time they want to use, because human beings are so completely wrapped up in the Intelligence that has come over them. They have become so unbelievably clever. Why, we are quite nervous to-day about the cleverness of the people we shall meet! We can scarcely ever escape from this anxiety, for nearly all of them are clever. Really we cannot escape from this anxiety about the cleverness of men. But of a truth the cleverness which is thus cultivated is used by Ahriman. And when moreover the bodies are especially adapted to a possible lowering or diminution of consciousness, it may happen that Ahriman himself emerges, incorporated in human form. Twice already it can be demonstrated that Ahriman has thus appeared as an author. And for those who desire as anthroposophists to have a clear and true vision of life, it will be a question of making no mistakes, even in such a case.

For what is the use of it, my dear friends, if someone finds a book somewhere and writes his name on it and he is not the author? The true author is confused with another. And if Ahriman is the author of a book, how can it be of any benefit if we do not perceive who is the true author, but hold a human being to be the author? For Ahriman by his brilliant gifts can find his way into everything—he can slip into the very style of a man. He has a way of approach to all things. What good can come of it if Ahriman is the real author, and we mistake it for a human work? To acquire the power of discrimination in this sphere too, is absolutely necessary, my dear friends.

I wanted to lead up to this point, describing thus in general a phenomenon which is also playing its part in our present age. In next Friday's lecture I shall have to speak of such phenomena in greater detail.

XI

Evolution of the Michael Principle Throughout the Ages

The Split in the Cosmic Intelligence

For a long time we have been speaking of the karmic facts and conditions connected with the Anthroposophical Movement, with the Anthroposophical Society and with the individuals who feel impelled out of an inner sincerity, to choose their path of life within this Movement. Much will remain to be said on these karmic questions after my return from England, but to-day, in our last lecture before my departure which will take me away for the rest of August,* to-day I would like to bring to a kind of conclusion what I have said. Thus in to-day's lecture we will to some extent round off the thoughts I have been able to communicate to you in these our studies upon karma.

You will all have observed, my dear friends, how manifold are the forms through which the karma of the individual anthroposophist has passed in former lives on earth and between death and a new birth. Especially in the last two

* The twenty-seven lectures given by Dr. Steiner in England (11th–30th August) were as follows:

In Torquay: *True and False Paths in Spiritual Investigation.* A course of eleven lectures published in English translation under this title: published in German under the title, *Das Initiaten-Bewusstsein.*

Course of seven lectures on *Education.*

Three lectures to Members of the Anthroposophical Society, published in English translation, together with those given in London, in the volume entitled, *Cosmic Christianity: Karma in the life of Individuals, and in the Evolution of the World.*

In London: Three lectures to Members (see above).

Two lectures for doctors and medical students: *The Art of Healing from the standpoint of Spiritual Science.*

Public lecture on Education (arranged by the Educational Union for the Realisation of Spiritual Values).

lectures we have been able to hint at the great significance which these things may have for the individual anthroposophist in his karma. We have seen how the karma of anthroposophists is connected with the evolution of the Michael principle through long, long epochs of time. To begin with, we saw in a more abstract form how the rulership of the Cosmic Intelligence—for so we called it—fell from the dominion of Michael. For as I said, in ancient times it was so indeed, that men could not ascribe to themselves the essence of Intelligence. They ascribed to the inspiration of higher Powers all that they could express in forms of Intelligence. And those who had knowledge of these matters knew that the higher Powers here concerned were the ones who afterwards, in Christian terminology, were designated as the Powers of Michael. I also spoke to you of the 8th or 9th century A.D. as the point of time in the evolution of civilised mankind when the Cosmic Intelligence gradually moved down to the earth, took shape as it were in many single drops which then lived on as personal Intelligence in single human souls. And I told you, my dear friends, how the perception and understanding of the Cosmic Intelligence—that is to say, of the old rulership by Michael, —lived on traditionally, with a certain reality of insight. We turn our gaze for instance to those, in many respects excellent, scholars who were connected with Arabism and with the Aristotelianism that had lived on in Asia since the campaigns of Alexander. This Aristotelianism had also permeated the mysticism of the East, filling it, as it were, with Intelligence. All this was carried across through Africa to Spain and went on working there, in the wisdom of the Moors, in such outstanding individualities as Averroes; and in the teachings of these Moorish, Spanish scholars we find a very real reflection of those old perceptions which had still looked upward to the Cosmic Intelligence.

Let us try to gain a vivid idea of how the Cosmic Intelligence had been conceived. I will give you a rough sketch of what these Moorish, Spanish scholars taught to their pupils in Spain in the 10th, 11th and 12th centuries, in the time when in other parts of Europe such things were prevailing as the School of Chartres, of which I have told you so much. In Spain it was taught by the Moorish scholars and above all by such an individuality as Averroes, that the Intelligence holds sway everywhere. The whole world, the whole cosmos is filled with the all-pervading Intelligence. Human beings down here on earth have many different properties, but they do not possess a personal intelligence of their own. On the contrary, every time a human being is active on the earth, a drop of Intelligence, a ray of Intelligence proceeds from the universal Intelligence, and descends as it were into the head, into the body of the single human being. So that the human being as he walks about on earth, shares in the universal Cosmic Intelligence which is common to all. And when he dies, when he passes through the gate of death, the Intelligence that was his returns to the universal Intelligence, flows back again. Thus all the thoughts, conceptions and ideas which man possesses in the life between birth and death flow back into the common reservoir of the universal Intelligence. One cannot therefore say that the thing of outstanding value in man's soul, namely his Intelligence, is subject to personal immortality. Indeed it was actually taught by the Spanish, Moorish scholars that man does not possess personal immortality. True, he lives on, but, said these scholars, the most important thing about him during his life is the fact that he can unfold intelligent knowledge, and this does *not* remain with his own being. We cannot therefore say that the intelligent being possesses personal immortality. You see, this was the very point in the fury of the battle which was waged by the Schoolmen of the Dominican Order. It was to maintain and uphold the personal immortality of man. And in that time, such a striving could appear in no other way than it did when the Dominicans declared: Man is personally immortal, and the teaching of Averroes on this subject is *heresy*, absolute heresy. To-day we have to put it differently, but for that time one can understand that a man like Averroes in Spain, who did not assume the personal immortality of man, was declared a heretic. To-day we have to study the matter in its reality. We have to say: In the sense in which man has become immortal, as to his Spiritual Soul, he has indeed attained immortality—the continued consciousness of personality after passing through the gate of death—but he has attained this only since the time when a Spiritual Soul took up its abode in earthly man. If therefore we had asked Aristotle or Alexander what were their thoughts about immortality, what would have been their answer? The words of course are not the point. But if, being asked, they had answered in our Christian terminology, they would have said: Our soul is received by Michael and we live on in the communion of Michael. Or they would have expressed it cosmologically. Above all in a community such as that of Alexander or Aristotle, they would have spoken thus in cosmic terms, and indeed they did speak thus: The soul of man is intelligent on earth, but this Intelligence is a drop out of the fulness of what Michael pours forth like a rain of Intelligence, flowing out over mankind. This rain proceeds from the Sun, and the Sun receives the human soul back again into its own being. The human soul as it exists between birth and death is rayed down to Earth from the Sun. Thus on the Sun they would have looked for the dominion of Michael, and such would have been their answer, cosmologically speaking.

These conceptions found their way into Asia, returned from Asia and flourished among the Moors in Spain at the very time when the Scholastic Philosophy rose up in defence of personal immortality. We must not say with the Schoolmen that this conception was an error, but we must say: The evolution of mankind brought with it the individual and personal immortality of man. And it was by the Dominican Schoolmen that this personal immortality was first emphasised, while on the other hand an ancient truth—one that was no longer true for that age in the evolution of the human race—was put forward in the Academies conducted by the Moors in Spain. For we to-day must not only be tolerant of our contemporaries. We must be tolerant of those who went on propagating ancient teachings. Such tolerance was not possible in that time. Hence it is important for us to repeat this to ourselves again and again: The personal immortality maintained by Dominican Schoolmen has only been true since the time when the Spiritual Soul slowly and gradually entered into mankind.

We can also describe these things in a fully Imaginative form. When a man dies in our time—a man who was really able, during his earthly life, to permeate his soul with true Intelligence—having gone through the gate of death, he looks back upon his past earthly life and sees it as an independent life on earth. In former centuries, man having passed through the gate of death, and looking back upon his earthly life, saw how the etheric body became dissolved in the cosmos. Then he passed through the realm of souls, living through the events again in backward order. Then he could say to himself: 'Thus Michael, through the Sun, administers what was mine before.' This is the great difference. But we can only understand such developments in evolution when we look behind the scenes of existence, perceiving the Spiritual behind the Material. We must see the outer events in mankind even as they are shaped and formed out of the spiritual world.

At this point, my dear friends, you must enter once more into all that I have now told you. Remember that with the 9th century A.D. the great crisis was accomplished: the Cosmic Intelligence came down among earthly men. This was the objective fact, this was actually taking place. And now transplant yourselves into the Sun-sphere, where Michael and his hosts were holding sway as I have described. For they had perceived the departure of Christ from the Sun and His passage to the earth in the Mystery of Golgotha, and after that, they had experienced how the Cosmic Intelligence descended more and more, to become individual human knowledge. Now there was one important event which made a deep impression, above all, on those who belong to Michael—whom in our last lecture I called the

'Michaelites.' It was an altogether outstanding event, which I have often described in other connections, showing the part it played in the unfolding of civilisation on the earth. Now, however, we must describe it as it appeared from the aspect of the Michaelites themselves, namely from the Sun. We must describe it as it is seen from that perspective—when one looks down from the realm of Michael on to the earth. This most significant event took place in the year 869 A.D. At the 8th Ecumenical Council held in that year at Constantinople, it was declared dogmatically that the old conception of Trichotomy, saying that man consists of body, soul and Spirit, is heretical. It was declared: Man has only body and soul, save that his soul possesses certain spiritual qualities. While in the sphere of objective realities the passage of the Intelligence into the single human beings was being accomplished, it was decreed on earth: Trichotomy is a false heresy. It was decreed in such a final and decisive form that no one within European civilisation could venture henceforth to contradict it. Henceforth one was forbidden to say that man has body, soul and Spirit. One might only speak of body and soul, ascribing spiritual qualities and forces to the soul. Something had thus taken place on earth, of which in the realms of Michael they could only say: Now there will enter into the souls of men the conviction that the Spiritual is but a quality of the soul, and not the Divine which holds sway in the great process of mankind's evolution. 'Look down upon the earth'—such was the language of Michael—'Look down upon the earth, behold the consciousness of the Spirit vanishing away.' But you must see, my dear friends, this vanishing of the consciousness of the Spirit was bound up with the main subject of which we wish to speak to-day.

As I said just now, hitherto I have only described in abstract terms how the evolution of the Michael realm has taken place behind the scenes of earth-existence. I have said: the Cosmic Intelligence came down to the single men. But this, my dear friends, is only an abstraction. For what *is* Intelligence? Needless to say we must not conceive that when we ascend into the higher regions we shall be able to take hold of the Intelligence there as we take hold of trees and shrubs here in the physical world. What is Intelligence? These abstract generalisations do not of course exist in reality. ' Intelligence ' means the mutual relationships of conduct among the higher Hierarchies. What *they* do, how they relate themselves to one another, what they are to one another,—this is the Cosmic Intelligence. And since as human beings we must first consider the kingdom that is nearest to us, concretely speaking the Cosmic Intelligence will be for us the sum-total of the Beings of the Hierarchy of Angeloi. If we are speaking concretely we cannot say ' so much Intelligence,' but rather ' so many Angeloi.' This is the reality.

When the Church Fathers were discussing in the year 869 A.D. whether man should speak henceforth of the Spirit, it was a consequence of the fact that a number of Angel Beings were separating from the realm of Michael where they had been before, and were assuming that they would henceforth have to do with earthly Powers only; —that the guidance of human beings would be achieved henceforth through earthly powers alone. You must see clearly what kind of an event this was. Angels are the Beings who guide men from earthly life to earthly life. They are the Beings next above us in the spiritual world, who lead us along our path in the life between death and a new birth and show us the way to our returning earthly life. They make of our several earthly lives a connected chain, a totality of human life. Now a number of Angel Beings—Beings who have this task and who had been united formerly with the Michael kingdom—went out and left the kingdom of Michael. Such being the conduct of these Angel Beings, the destiny of human beings could not possibly remain untouched. Who is it partakes in the very first place in the unfolding of human karma—in the way the earthly thoughts, the earthly deeds and earthly feelings are transformed and elaborated between death and a new birth? It is the Beings of the Angeloi. If now these Angel

Beings come to an entirely different position in the cosmos—if, so to speak, they leave the kingdom of the Sun and become no longer celestial Angels but terrestrial—what then must happen? Here we come upon a secret, permeating the whole evolution and history of Europe, hidden behind the external facts. Certain Angeloi remained in the kingdom of Michael. In that great School in the beginning of the 15th century we find also the Angel Beings belonging to the human beings who were then in the kingdom of Michael. To all the souls of human beings who lived in the kingdom of Michael and of whom I have spoken to you, belong Angel Beings who have remained in Michael's kingdom. But there were others who left it and identified themselves with that which was in essence earthly.

Now you will say: How is it possible that it suddenly occurs to a number of Michael Angels to leave the kingdom of Michael? It does not occur to the others to leave.—This, my dear friends, I must admit, is one of the most difficult questions that can possibly be raised in connection with the modern evolution of mankind. It is a question such that as we enter into it all the inner forces of the human being are called into play. It is a question deeply and intimately connected with the whole life of man. For you see, at the foundation of it there lies a cosmic fact. You know, from lectures I have given here, that what is commonly referred to as a mere physical planet is in reality a gathering of Spiritual Beings. When we look up to a star, that which appears to us physically is but the external aspect. In reality we have to do with a gathering of Spiritual Beings. Now there is a certain contrast. Since the very beginning of earthly evolution, this contrast has existed. It is the contrast between the Intelligences of all the planets and the Intelligence of the Sun. There is indeed on the one hand the Sun Intelligence, while on the other there are the Intelligences of the several planets. And it was always so, that the Sun Intelligence stood paramountly under the dominion of Michael, while the other Planetary Intelligences were subject to the other Archangels. Thus we may say:

Sun Intelligence.	Planetary Intelligences.	
Michael.	Mercury ...	... Raphael
	Venus ...	... Anael
	Mars ...	... Samael
	Jupiter ...	... Zachariel
	Moon ...	... Gabriel
	Saturn ...	... Oriphiel

On the other hand it was always so that one might not say, Michael administers the Sun Intelligence alone, but rather, Michael administers the whole Cosmic Intelligence, differentiated as it is into the Sun Intelligence and the Planetary Intelligences, Mercury, Venus, Mars, etc. The several Beings of the Hierarchy of Archangeloi partake in its administration. But over all of them together Michael holds sway ever and again. Thus the whole Cosmic Intelligence is administered by Michael. Now of course, every human being was a human being even before, when Michael administered the Cosmic Intelligence from which only a ray descended into the human individual. And it was due to the Sun that man on earth could yet feel himself as man; could feel himself as single man and not as a mere vehicle for the common Cosmic Intelligence. All human Intelligence comes from Michael in the Sun.

But when these centuries approached—the 8th, the 9th, the 10th century A.D.—it happened that the Planetary Intelligences began to reckon with the fact that the earth had changed, and that the Sun too had changed.

My dear friends, that which goes on externally, which the astronomers describe, is after all only the outer side. You know that approximately every 11 years we have a period of Sun-spots, when in the shining of the Sun upon the earth certain places are darkened, covered with spots or blotches. This was not always so. In very ancient times the Sun shone down as a uniform disc of light. There were no Sun-spots. Moreover, after some thousands of years the Sun will have very many more spots than it has to-day. The Sun is growing ever more spotted. This again is the outer manifestation of the fact that the Michael Power, the Cosmic Power of Intelligence is still decreasing. In the increase of the Sun-spots in the course of Cosmic Evolution is revealed the Sun's decay; the Sun within the cosmos grows increasingly dim and old. And at the appearance of a sufficiently large number of Sun-spots, the other Planetary Intelligences recognised that they would now no longer be ruled by the Sun. They resolved no longer to allow the earth to be dependent on the Sun, but to make it dependent henceforth on the entire cosmos directly. This took place through the planetary Counsels of the Archangels. Notably under the leadership of Oriphiel, this emancipation of the Planetary Intelligences from the Sun-Intelligence took place. It was a complete separation of Cosmic Powers that had hitherto belonged together. The Sun-Intelligence of Michael and the Planetary Intelligences gradually came into cosmic opposition one with another.

Yes, my dear friends, though we do ascribe an entirely different kind of inner nature—of soul-faculty and soul-condition—to the Beings of the Hierarchy of the Angeloi, nevertheless we must ascribe *decisions*, weighty *reflections* on that which is taking place, even to them. For we human beings also make our decisions in no other way. We observe the things that are taking place externally before us, we let the facts speak for themselves and then, under the influence of the facts, we act accordingly. Only the determining factors for us between birth and death are earthly facts, whereas for the Beings of the Hierarchy of Angeloi they are cosmic facts, as when a split takes place in the planetary life.

Thus the one host of Beings turned to the Earth-Intelligence and therewith at the same time to the Planetary Intelligence. The other host remained true to the sphere of Michael in order to carry into all the future what Michael administers as the Eternal. And this is the decisive question to-day. Now that all the power is among men, will Michael be able to carry into all the future that which is Eternal in his working,—now that that which appears in the physical Sun grows darker and vanishes slowly away?

Thus we see, as an outcome of cosmic events, a split among

the Angeloi who were formerly united with Michael. But these Beings themselves partake in the karmic evolution. Consider the whole of this as it takes place in the life between death and a new birth. Here it is not so that every human soul can run his course alone, nor can every Angel who guides the human being run his course alone, but the Hierarchy of Angeloi work together; and in their working-together karma lives and is worked out. If in an earthly life I become connected with another human being and we work this out karmically in our next life, then, needless to say, the Angel of the one human being must come together with the Angel of the other. A co-operation must take place. But in many cases this was what happened (and this is the overwhelming, shattering experience). In the Ecumenical Council that took place on earth in 869 A.D. the signal was given for an overwhelming event in the spiritual world above. It would almost shatter one to pieces, when one holds oneself entirely upright with the true use of the Cosmic Intelligence, face to face with such overpowering relationships. It is a thing of untold significance that has already happened and is happening more and more: the Angel of the one human being, of the one human soul who was karmically connected with another human soul, did not go on with the Angel of that other soul. Of two human souls karmically united with one another, the one Angel remained with Michael while the other went down to earth. What was bound to happen as a result? In the time between the founding of Christianity and the age of the Spiritual Soul, which is signalised above all by the 9th century and the year 869 A.D., the karma of human beings came into disorder. This is to pronounce one of the deepest and most important words that can possibly be uttered with regard to the modern history of mankind. Disorder came into the karma of present-day humanity. In the following lives on earth the experiences of men were no longer all of them rightly co-ordinated with their karma. This is the chaotic element in the history of recent times. This has brought into the history of recent times more and more social chaos, chaos of civilisation; and the disorder that has come into human karma can find no end. For a split has taken place in the Hierarchy of Angeloi belonging to Michael.

And now we may express something that is deeply connected with the karma of the Anthroposophical Society. It is a thing of immense significance, and, if I may say so, it is only here that we come to the right shade of feeling. For with all that we *can* describe by choosing comparisons from the conditions that surround us, we cannot exhaustively characterise what is taking place behind the scenes in spiritual worlds. Whatever thoughts we may select from the earthly conditions that surround us, they are but dim and feeble. Having made all these preparations, we must have recourse to the pure description of things spiritual.

Thus we must say: All that has led the souls together into the Anthroposophical Society, all that has brought them into this community through a sincere and inward impulse of their souls, holds good, needless to say. Yet how does it come about? How are the forces really there, which lead these human beings in our time to find their way together under purely spiritual principles, when in the ordinary world of to-day they are complete strangers to one another? Where do the forces lie, that lead them together? My dear friends, they lie in this: Through the entry of Michael's dominion in the Michael age in which we live—with the penetration of Michael to earthly rulership, replacing the rulership of Gabriel—Michael himself is bringing the power which is to bring order again into the karma of those who have gone with him. Thus we may say: What is it in the last resort that unites the Members of the Anthroposophical Society? It is that they are to bring order again into their karma. This unites them. And if any one of them notices in the course of his life that he is entering here or there into relationships that do not conform to his inmost impulse,—relationships, perhaps, diverging in one way or another from what we may call the true harmony in man as between good and evil,—if he has this on the one hand, while on the other hand he has constant impulse to press forward in the

Anthroposophical life,—the fact is that such a man is striving back again to his real karma. He is striving once more to live and express the real karma. This is the cosmic ray that pours through the Anthroposophical Movement, clearly perceptible to him who knows. It is *the restoration of the truth in karma.*

In this connection we can understand very much, both of the destiny of individuals in the Anthroposophical Society and of the destiny of the whole Society. For these, of course, merge into one another.

We must also realise the following: For the human beings who are connected with those Beings of the Hierarchy of Angeloi who remained in the kingdom of Michael, it is difficult to find the forms of Intelligence adequate to that which they are now to understand. They are striving to maintain even the personal Intelligence in keeping with the true reverence for Michael. These souls, who as I told you partook in those spiritual preparations in the 15th and 19th centuries, come down to earth, devoted still, with their deepest inner striving, to Michael and to his sphere. And yet, in accordance with the principles of human evolution, they must receive the personal and individual Intelligence. The result is a split, a division which must however be solved by spiritual development. They, in their individual affinity, must come together with what the spiritual worlds are bringing down to them in the present age of Intelligence. Those on the other hand whose Angels fell away (which is of course connected with their karma, for the Angel falls if he is connected with a human karma that is according to this)—they receive their personal Intelligence as a complete matter of course. This means that it works in them automatically, through their bodily nature. It works in such a way that they think, think cleverly, but are not fully and deeply and humanly concerned in what they think. This indeed was the great conflict which lasted so long, between the Dominicans and the Franciscans. The Dominicans could not evolve the principle of personal Intelligence otherwise than in the greatest possible faithfulness to the sphere of Michael. But the Franciscans, the followers of Duns Scotus (not Scotus Erigena) became complete Nominalists. They said: Intelligence in any case is only so many words. All that happened in these discussions and arguments between men was in reality an image of mighty conflicts that took place between the one host of Angeloi and the other.

You see, it is so, that the Beings of the Hierarchy of Angeloi who have now united themselves with the earth-principle, have been living on the earth, in a manner of speaking, since about the 9th or 10th century. This again is the shattering tragedy, my dear friends. Here upon earth, materialism is increasing. The human beings—and above all the most advanced, the cleverest among them—are of such a kind as to deny the Spiritual. They begin to laugh in scorn at the idea that Spiritual Beings should be in their environment no less than physical human beings. During this time in which materialism has been expanding on the earth, more and more Angels are descending and living on the earth. They themselves join in; for it was they who at certain times, when a human consciousness became impaired and dull, incorporated themselves and worked on earth. A large number of Angeloi-Beings refrain and hold themselves aloof; but those who by their karma as Angeloi stand nearest to the Ahrimanic powers, do not hold back; at certain times they incorporate themselves in men; they dive down into human beings.

Then there arises what I described in our last lecture, when I said: Here now is such a man on earth. He has great human talent, human Intelligence, which he expresses, maybe, with genius. But for a certain time when his consciousness is dimmed, an Ahrimanic Angeloi-Intelligence takes up his abode in him. At such a time, this may occur: There is the human being; he seems as though he were an ordinary human being, writing this or that out of his own humanity. (Now Ahriman can approach the human being most easily through the very things which the men of to-day receive in the forms of Intelligence. One must assert one's personality fully, if one is not to be engulfed to-day in all those things that I have indicated in the course of the last lectures). Hence it is that Ahriman can appear as an author. He makes use, of course, of an Angelos-Being. He can write like an author. And as we are now united in the sign of our Christmas Foundation Meeting, we will not be silent on these things. Therefore I will now add the following.

A very different attitude was possible to one of the most brilliant authors of recent times, one of the greatest authors —a very different attitude was possible before his last works appeared. When I wrote my book *Nietzsche, a Wrestler with his Time*, all that had come before the public was Nietzsche the brilliant writer, a man who had carried human faculties to the highest point of eminence. It was only afterwards that one became acquainted with what Nietzsche wrote in the period of his decay. There are above all the two works *Anti-Christ* and *Ecce Homo*. These two works were written by Ahriman and not by Nietzsche. It was an Ahrimanic spirit incorporated in Nietzsche. Here it was, for the first time,that Ahriman appeared as an author upon earth. He will continue to do so. Nietzsche broke down over it. He went to pieces. We must understand the true nature of the impulses we are confronting when we stand face to face with the ideas that lived in Nietzsche in the time when he wrote the brilliant but devilish works *Anti-Christ* and *Ecce Homo*, —intelligent works indeed. I have spoken of the great and all-embracing Intelligence of Ahriman. For greatness, majesty and brilliance, we do not decry a work in calling it Ahrimanic. Only simpletons could think so, who do not know the greatness there can be in Ahriman. We do not blame when we speak of Ahriman. Very much on earth depends on him. I can truly say that in my soul I bled, when for the first time I read Nietzsche's writing on the 'Will to Power,' which was then published in such a way that men could gain no right conception of it. But if at the same time one is able to look into those kingdoms which since the dominion of Michael, since the eighties of last century, were severed by the thinnest of thin walls from the earth-kingdom; if one knows how immediately this kingdom adjoins the physical, so that we may say: ' It is a kingdom similar to that which man passes through after his death '; if one can gaze into these things and see how great the strivings are in this direction, then too one knows with what impulsive power they are coming to expression in such a thing as the *Ecce Homo* and the *Anti-Christ*. We need only consider how Ahrimanic are the remarks that occur in the *Anti-Christ*. I do not know whether the passage is still in the same form in the more recent editions. There is a passage where he is writing on Jesus. (I am not quoting verbatim). He says: Renan describes Jesus as a genius. Nietzsche does not see him as a genius, for he goes on to say: Speaking with the strict accuracy of a psychologist we should use a very different word . . . In my edition of Nietzsche's works there are three dots at this point. I do not know whether it is so in the newer editions too, but in the manuscript there stands at this point the word ' idiot,' written in full. That Jesus is described as an ' idiot,' this is the hand of Ahriman. And many other things of this kind stand written there. We must remember that at the very time when he was writing these things, there were tendencies in Nietzsche's soul towards Catholicism. We must not forget that these things went parallel with one another. Who, knowing this, could fail to think that a deep riddle lies hidden there? And what are the concluding words of the *Anti-Christ*? They are somewhat as follows, though again I am not quoting verbatim: ' I would like to write it on every wall and I have the materials to write it in radiant letters shining far and wide; I would fain write what Christianity is. It is the greatest curse of mankind.'—Thus ends the book. Surely here lies a problem. We must see indeed, how that kingdom which was separated by a thin wall only from our own, and where all the spiritual battles took place towards the end and a little beyond the end of Kali Yuga—we must see how that kingdom is striving to penetrate into the physical domain of earth.

To these things we must look if we would understand

what can be the position of mankind to-day, towards the things that must emerge in civilisation through the dawn of the age of Michael. At the transition of the Kali Yuga—the transition from the dark to the light age—one did indeed have to see things clearly, graphically, in the spiritual and in the physical together, if one would describe (as I did in the Introduction to my *Mysticism at the Dawn of the Modern Spiritual Life*) the necessary feeling at that time towards the Spiritual and the Material. From all directions one would like to gather the means of expression to describe the mighty transition that takes place at the dawn of the Michael age. And with all that the Anthroposophical Movement is, we must feel ourselves within these things. For all these mighty, overwhelming facts express themselves to begin with in the human karma which has now come into disorder. We must think of the great and universal truth that lies inherent in the karmic relationships. Yet the world to-day is such that even into these general karmic laws and relationships, exceptions could enter through the course of many centuries. And now the requirement is to bring these cosmic exceptions back into their true course. If we think of these things—for this is the task, the mission of the Anthroposophical Movement,—we shall feel something of the great and far-reaching significance of this Movement.

This, my dear friends, shall now rest in your souls. You must say to yourselves: Those who out of these great decisions feel in themselves the impulse to come to the anthroposophical life to-day, will be called again at the end of the 20th century, when at the culminating point the greatest possible expansion of the Anthroposophical Movement will be attained. But it will only happen if these things can really live in us,—if there can live in us the perception of what penetrates cosmically, spiritually, into the earthly physical domain. It will only be so if there penetrates even into the earthly Intelligence, into the perceptions of men, the knowledge of the significance of Michael.

This impulse must be the very soul of our anthroposophical striving. The soul itself must have the will to stand fully in the midst of the Anthroposophical Movement. Thus we shall find it possible, my dear friends, for a certain time to come, to carry in our souls thoughts of a great and far-reaching nature. But we shall not only preserve them, we shall make them living in our souls. And through these thoughts our souls will grow and develop anthroposophically, so that the soul will *become* what it was intended to become through its own unconscious impulse to come to Anthroposophy. I say again: So that the soul may be *taken hold of* by the mission of Anthroposophy. I have spoken these earnest words to you in this last hour, so that you may let them work in you quietly and in silence for a time: that the soul shall really be taken hold of by the mission of Anthroposophy. We shall continue these lessons when we come together again,—that will be in the first days of September. For the intervening time I would like to have laid on all your hearts what I have had to say this evening in connection with the karma of individual anthroposophists and of the Anthroposophical Society.

Publisher's Note Regarding Rudolf Steiner's Lectures

The lectures contained in this volume have been translated from the German which is based on stenographic and other recorded texts that were in most cases never seen or revised by the lecturer. Hence, due to human errors in hearing and transcription, they may contain mistakes and faulty passages. Every effort has been made to ensure that this is not the case. Some of the lectures were given to audiences more familiar with anthroposophy; these are the so-called 'private' or 'members' lectures. Other lectures, like the written works, were intended for the general public. The differences between these, as Rudolf Steiner indicates in his *Autobiography*, is twofold. On the one hand, the members' lectures take for granted a background in and commitment to anthroposophy; in the public lectures this was not the case. At the same time, the members' lectures address the concerns and dilemmas of the members, while the public work speaks directly out of Steiner's own understanding of universal needs. Nevertheless, as Rudolf Steiner stresses: 'Nothing was ever said that was not solely the result of my direct experience of the growing content of anthroposophy. There was never any question of concessions to the prejudices and preferences of the members. Whoever reads these privately printed lectures can take them to represent anthroposophy in the fullest sense. Thus it was possible without hesitation—when the complaints in this direction became too persistent—to depart from the custom of circulating this material "for members only". But it must be borne in mind that faulty passages do occur in these reports not revised by myself.' Earlier in the same chapter, he states: 'Had I been able to correct them [the private lectures] the restriction [for members only] would have been unnecessary from the beginning.'

Karmic Relationships
Esoteric Studies

The full series, now available:

Volume 1
Features an overview of the laws and conditions of karma, and goes on to consider the incarnations of Friedrich Nietzsche, Lord Bacon of Verulam, Lord Byron and many others.
Trans: G. Adams, rev. M. Cotterell, C. Davy & D. S. Osmond (12 lectures, Dornach, 16 Feb–23 Mar 1924, GA 235); 206pp; ISBN 0 85440 260 8

Volume 2
Features individual karmic relationships in history—for example Marx and Engels—as well as a survey of karma in human life, the shaping of karma after death, and the 'cosmic form' of karma.
Trans: G. Adams, rev. M. Cotterell, C. Davy & D. S. Osmond (16 lectures, Dornach, 6 Apr–29 Jun 1924, GA 236); 256pp; ISBN 0 85440 281 0

Volume 3
The Karmic Relationships of the Anthroposophical Movement. Includes predispositions which lead souls to anthroposophy, the two streams within the movement, plus Rosicrucianism, Arabism, Aristotelianism, the Platonists and the School of Michael.
Trans: G. Adams, rev. D. S. Osmond (11 lectures, Dornach, 1 Jul to 8 Aug 1924, GA 237); 180pp; ISBN 0 85440 313 2

Volume 4
The karmic groups of souls connected to Aristotelianism and Platonism, the karma of the anthroposophical movement, as well as the individual incarnations of Ernst Haeckel, Vladimir Solovioff and others. This new edition also includes Steiner's last address.
Trans: G. Adams, C. Davy & D. S. Osmond (11 lectures, Dornach, 5–24 Sept 1924, GA 238); 174pp; ISBN 0 85440 412 0

Volume 5

The difference between 'moon karma' and 'sun karma', the influences of Christian and Mohammedan thinking, the transformation of inner human qualities from one life to the next, and much more.

Trans: D. S. Osmond (7 lectures, Prague & Paris, 29 Mar–25 May 1924, GA 239); 112pp; ISBN 0 85440 432 5

Volume 6

A study of the karma of the anthroposophical movement and society, the spiritual gates of the sun and moon, and much more.

Trans: D. S. Osmond (9 lectures, various cities, 25 Jan–20 Jul 1924, GA 235, 236, 240); 184pp; ISBN 0 85440 242 X

Volume 7

Human experiences after death and before a new birth; karma in world history; the cosmic nature of Christ; waking, dreaming, sleeping; the physical effects of karma, etc.

Trans: D. S. Osmond (9 lectures, Breslau, 7–15 Jun 1924, GA 239); 144pp; ISBN 0 85440 276 4

Volume 8

Subjects include Cosmic Christianity, the Michael impulse, the Arthur and Grail streams of wisdom, plus Gregory VII, Haeckel, Swedenborg, Loyola, Haroun al Raschid, Byron, Voltaire and others.

Trans: D. S. Osmond (6 lectures, Torquay 12–21 Aug, London 24–27Aug 1924, GA 240); 102pp; ISBN 0 85440 018 4